SPITFIRE PILOT

"Flight Lieutenant Crook reads like a Battle of Britain blog. This diary of a Spitfire Pilot puts the reader in the cockpit, fighting for the nation's survival. The reader shares his elation at winning the battle of the skies, but also his sorrow at the loss of so many friends. One colleague accurately describes his pilot's wings as a 'one way ticket'. The reader will share the excitement of a scramble which takes just ninety seconds from deckchair to Spitfire on the move. To relive the triumphs, the fun and the downs of a Battle of Britain pilot read this book."

Air Marshal The Lord Garden, K.C.B.

SPITFIRE PILOT

A Personal Account of the Battle of Britain

Flight Lieutenant D. M. Crook, D.F.C.

Introduction by Richard Overy

ISIS
LARGE PRINT
Oxford

First published in Great Britain 1942
by
Faber

Published in Large Print 2009 by ISIS Publishing Ltd.,
7 Centremead, Osney Mead, Oxford OX2 0ES
by arrangement with
Casemate

British Library Cataloguing in Publication Data
Crook, D. M. (David Moore)
    Spitfire pilot [text (large print)]. - - (Reminiscence)
    1. Crook, D. M. (David Moore)
    2. Great Britain. Royal Air Force. Squadron, 609.
    3. Britain, Battle of, Great Britain, 1940.
    4. World War, 1939–1945 - - Aerial operations,
    British.
    5. World War, 1939–1945 - - Personal narratives,
    British.
    6. Spitfire (Fighter planes)
    7. Large type books.
    I. Title II. Series
    940.5'4211'092–dc22

ISBN 978–0–7531–8342–7 (hb)
ISBN 978–0–7531–8343–4 (pb)

Printed and bound in Great Britain by
T. J. International Ltd., Padstow, Cornwall

Contents

PREFACE

By all accounts my father, David Moore Crook, had two overriding passions in his life — his flying and his family. I say "by all accounts" because he died in December 1944. *Spitfire Pilot* therefore is the voice of the father that my brother, sister and I do not remember, and yet whom we feel to know so well. The book started as a personal diary, kept with the intention of recording impressions and emotions at the time, as a sort of time capsule. Some of David's fellow officers persuaded him to try to have it published, but this was not in his mind at the time of writing, and the wording remains true to the original document.

David was the eldest child of Clifford and Winifred Crook, born on 24th November 1914 in Huddersfield, where he grew up at Glenwood, the family house so often mentioned in his diary. Writing, reading and diary-keeping were part and parcel of family life; indeed three of his family read English at Oxford. Clifford Crook had inherited a business which he developed into a very successful sports goods manufacturing company, of which the Mitre football was the most famous product. During World War II the whole of the Huddersfield factory was turned over to supplying the aircraft industry.

As business fluctuated in the early days of their marriage David's parents experienced "both feast and famine". Family values reflected their situation and their church-going Yorkshire backgrounds. These included the importance of strength of character, the Ten Commandments, lifelong learning, prudence with money — and good table manners! This rather austere description does not do justice to the sparkle within the family. Clifford's 1959 obituary described him as a man of abundant vitality and philanthropy, with a gift for inspiring others.

The family's early holidays were spent by the sea at Thornwick Bay, and it was here that my father first became fascinated by flight as he watched the sea birds skimming over the coastline. Other holidays were in Switzerland or in the Lake District. David loved the outdoors, sometimes in quiet contemplation of the countryside — and at other times in adventurous pursuits such as rock climbing or tackling the Cresta Run with his father and brothers.

It was while he was still at school that David took his first flying lessons. David and his brother Paul, along with their great childhood friend Geoff Gaunt, were educated at The Leys, Cambridge from the mid-1920s. Friendships forged at that time included those with Maurice Berry and Gordon Mitchell. In later years Paul was to marry Maurice's sister, Katharine, and Geoff and Gordon were to join 609 Squadron with David.

After leaving school David joined the family business, working his way up from the bottom and in due course becoming a director. However he harboured aspirations of eventually moving from industry into politics. Meanwhile his love of flying persisted, and in 1938 he joined the Auxiliary Air Force and was assigned to 609 (West Riding) Squadron. It was at this time too that he met Dorothy "D." Middleton, daughter of an Anglican clergyman, who was nursing at St Thomas's Hospital. Eight months later they were to marry by special licence on the eve of the declaration of war. A year later he wrote in his diary: "I am not including anything personal about Dorothy or myself, except to say that, despite the war and all its inevitable worry and anxiety, this year since our marriage has been by far the happiest year of my life. And that is saying a very great deal, since all those years have been so happy."

It is a great bonus now to be able to read his diary in conjunction with the letters he wrote and the stories that family and friends recall, giving such an insight into the man he was. In writing this piece I owe particular thanks to Derek Price, who flew with David; to David Darley, Hugh Mulligan and Mark Crame of 609 Squadron Association, to my aunt Katharine Crook, and especially to my brother Nicholas Crook and sister Elizabeth Tapsell for papers and photographs. Many have commented on David's gifts of leadership, and for including and encouraging those on the perimeter. He was also the most devoted and practical father. After the Battle of Britain he was posted in November 1940 to become an instructor, and he records at the end of the book his dismay at having to leave behind his beloved R6699 Spitfire on 609 Squadron. In private notes he wrote "This has been the most exhilarating, exciting and yet tragic six months." In the same week he describes the joy of greeting his firstborn child Nicholas, of which he wrote: "That was the best moment I ever had."

In April 1944 David joined an Advanced Flying Unit and by November was on his way back to an operational squadron, to be Squadron Leader from January 1945. However, before taking up that post, he was one of eighteen pilots who were posted to Scotland for training in high-level photographic reconnaissance.

Before leaving he came home where Dorothy had recently given birth to my younger sister, Elizabeth "Wizzie", and Nicholas was celebrating his fourth birthday. A few days later David wrote home to reassure Dorothy that the rumours of dangers associated with the course were unfounded, that he was settling in and that on this, the sixth anniversary of their meeting, he loved her more than ever. A fortnight later, on 18th December 1944, on a clear morning David flew off to exercise in the local area. He returned to base with a technical problem before setting off again. Shortly afterwards a local coastguard reported seeing an aircraft go straight into the North Sea from some 30,000 feet. David did not return and his body was never recovered. No one will ever know what happened, but at the time it was supposed that his oxygen had failed in some way. I believe a total of six pilots were lost during the six-week course. The name of David Moore Crook D.F.C. is inscribed on Panel 202 of the R.A.F. memorial to the missing at Runnymede. The friend and fellow-pilot, Derek Price, who breakfasted with David on that last morning wrote the following for an article in 1980:

David was one of the nicest people I have ever known — a very good and loyal friend — a very interesting and amusing person to spend time with and a very courageous man. I shall always count it an honour to have been numbered among his many friends and he was an inspiration to all of us at a time when it was so easy to get downhearted. It was a terrible waste that he should have been killed in the way he was, having been through so much during the Battle of Britain. Even today, so many years after, I remember him very vividly and perhaps the best way to finish these few reminiscences is to say that he was certainly one of the best of his generation.

My mother has often talked of how much my father appreciated the support of the allied pilots in the R.A.F., and in the bleak post-war days we received parcels of food treats from New Zealanders who had known him. The story continues into the present day. In 1998 the propeller of a Messerschmidt Bf109 E, found in a scrap-yard, was identified as belonging to an aircraft shot down by David Crook on 13th August 1940 over Poole Harbour. Records show that the German pilot was held as a P.O.W. until the end of the war. The Mayor of Poole held a reception in honour of my father which was attended by my brother and his wife. The following year we received a letter from the nephew of Tadeusz "Novi" Nowierski, one of David's Polish friends in 609 Squadron, and who went on to become a Group Captain after his distinguished war service:

I have at long last been able to trace you because I want very much to say your father will always be dearly remembered. He saved the life of Novi by warning him not to land on one wheel. Neither will your father be forgotten for his heartfelt and eloquent tribute made to Polish pilots who in those difficult times so gratefully accepted his words of solace. He will always be remembered as a true friend of Poland and his name has its permanent place in the annals of the Polish Air Force.

In September 2005 Prince Charles unveiled the Battle of Britain Memorial on London's Victoria Embankment, where all the names of those who fought in the Battle of Britain are commemorated. And nearby in Lambeth at the Imperial War Museum is displayed the Spitfire in which my father flew on 609 (WR) Squadron, designed of course by R. J. Mitchell.

Perhaps the best encapsulation of what it meant to be a fighter pilot is found in the verses of *Between Midnight and Morning* by Owen Seaman (1861–1936) which are written in my father's hand in the back of my mother's copy of *Spitfire Pilot:*

You that have faith to look with fearless eyes
Beyond the tragedy of a world at strife
And trust that of night and death shall rise
The dawn of ampler life;

Rejoice, whatever anguish rend your heart,
That God has given you, for a priceless dower
To live in these great times and have your part
In Freedom's crowning hour.

That you may tell your sons who see the light
High in the heaven, their heritage to take:
"I saw the powers of darkness put to flight!
I saw the morning break!"

Rosemary Loyd
2006

ON 609 SQUADRON

Spitfire Pilot is a volume that has long had a place of honour on my bookshelves, a treasure found like so many literary gems in a second-hand bookshop. I was therefore delighted to be told that it was to be published again, over sixty-five years since the events so graphically described in its pages. D. M. Crook writes with a modesty that becomes him yet does full justice to the "band of brothers" that formed 609 (West Riding) Squadron of the Auxiliary Air Force at the outbreak of war.

This is a story of almost unimaginable courage and skill, at a time when both these qualities were so badly needed by our nation. But he writes, too, of the family that was the squadron and of the highs and lows of emotion felt by its members as they experienced both success and tragedy. Also their reliance on their ground crews does not go unnoticed and he writes touchingly on the comradeship placed by him and others on these devoted toilers. He would recognise much the same spirit in the members of today's 609 which — although it is no longer a fighter squadron — has performed superbly in support of the regular Royal Air Force.

Those serving today on 609 are deeply proud of their Squadron's distinguished history, so gloriously begun by "D.M.C." and his peers. I think that he would feel at home in their company and with the older members of the Squadron Association.

No. 609 (West Riding) Squadron of the Auxiliary Air Force was formed a little over sixty-five years ago at Yeadon Aerodrome, today's Leeds Bradford Airport, under the command of Squadron Leader Harald Peake. It was the latest in what would be a force of twenty-one squadrons, raised in the traditions of local volunteer service. Its aims were similar to those of the Territorial Army, principally to offer a substantial reserve of trained, formed units, capable of reinforcing and of fighting alongside the relatively small regular services of the day. The expansion of the Auxiliary Air Force in 1936 reflected concerns about the burgeoning strength of Hitler's Germany, and by the outbreak of war, both the anti-aircraft gunners of the T.A. and the fighter squadrons of the A.A.F. would be expected to play a significant part in the defence of the realm.

This, then, was the climate of world affairs when Pilot Officer D. M. Crook was commissioned as a trainee pilot in November 1938, shortly after the Munich Crisis and only a month before 609 was designated a fighter squadron. As his flying training began, the Squadron was to receive its first Spitfires, just in time for the outbreak of war on the 3rd September 1939.

In what may be considered the world's first integrated air defence system, the fighter squadrons of the A.A.F. fought shoulder to shoulder with their regular counterparts. R.A.F. Fighter Command's Commander-in-Chief, Sir Hugh Dowding, had created a control network that gave our airborne fighter pilots the benefit of up to the minute information about where enemy formations were to be found. The sky is a vast place and without such help, largely the result of the creation of a radar chain that provided accurate early warning, the result of the Battle of Britain would have been very different.

D. M. Crook describes 609's part in the air battles of summer 1940 simply and with great clarity. He reveals the courage and dash of his fellow pilots and the depth of support that they relied upon, from their own ground personnel and from the great air defence system that allowed Operations Rooms to pinpoint the enemy's position. 609's story was an especially glorious one and owed much to the leadership of the Commanding Officer of the day, Squadron Leader H. S. Darley. By October 1940, no fewer than 100 enemy aircraft had fallen to the guns of 609's aircraft, a record rarely surpassed, even by regular units.

D. M. Crook left 609 Squadron in November 1940 to become a flying instructor and plainly found leaving a wrench. He was one of only a few pre-war members left — many having been killed in action or posted away. Like other A.A.F. squadrons, 609 inevitably changed in character and depended on its remaining auxiliary ground crew members to keep alight its intense pride in its origins. That pride communicated itself to succeeding generations of squadron members, notably a substantial contingent of Belgian pilots who served with distinction later in the war. One of these contingents introduced perhaps its most notorious member, Pilot Officer William de Goat, a mascot who survived the war and a meteoric rise to the rank of Air Commodore, besides numerous indiscretions along the way. He is preserved in life-sized effigy to this day, a proud reminder of the wartime Squadron!

In 1942, re-equipped with the Hawker Typhoon, 609 Squadron excelled in the ground attacks in the aftermath of D-Day, particularly in the killing ground of the Falaise Gap, which graphically illustrated the potency of air power and its influence over the land battle.

Soon after the war had ended, 609 Squadron was disbanded, but it was soon resurrected again and reformed at its ancestral home in Yeadon as a night fighter squadron. Two years later, it reverted to the day fighter role — and to the Spitfire. It entered the jet age in 1950, moving to Church Fenton, near Selby, which was destined to be its last home as a fighter squadron.

In 1957 came the body blow of disbandment again. At a stroke, all the fighter squadrons of the now Royal Auxiliary Air Force were stood down. For many, that sounded the death knell of 609 and it would take over 40 years for the historic squadron "number plate" to emerge from modest enhancements to the R.A.F.'s order of battle. Not long before yet another disbandment, 609 Squadron won the highly coveted Esher Trophy, awarded to the most efficient auxiliary squadron.

No. 609 (West Riding) Squadron was then reformed at R.A.F. Leeming in 2000, to provide ground support for the Royal Air Force, a role that it has performed with distinction, notably in the Gulf. The outbreak of hostilities in the Gulf, on 20th March 2003, saw no fewer than sixty members of 609 called up for service in Kuwait, Qatar, Cyprus, Jordan and Oman. These included five officers and fourteen N.C.O.s. The majority of the Squadron found themselves at Ali Al Salem airbase in Kuwait where they formed an integral part of the "Force Protection" for the Tornado aircraft operating from the base. From the outset, they came under missile attack and showed the same steadiness under fire that their forebears had done in the Second World War. Whereas in 1936 the membership of the Squadron was drawn from within a radius of 10 miles from the centre of Leeds, those deployed in 2003 represented most of the North of England.

Today, the members of 609 (West Riding) Squadron are established specialists in the Force Protection role and support the Royal Air Force by the provision of fluid ground defence, requiring infantry skills of the highest order. In addition, they are trained in the very technical disciplines of "C.B.R.N." defence — providing warning and protection against chemical, biological, radiological and nuclear threats.

Today's members have formed close and enthusiastic links with the 609 Squadron Association, the senior member of which is "Old Number One", Jim Thompson, who was the first Auxiliary airman to enlist in 1936. The Squadron has also played a part in reviving operational contact with the Belgian Air Force with which it recently exercised. Its members are very conscious of the Squadron's history and proud of its traditions. This new edition of *Spitfire Pilot* will be warmly welcomed by all of us who have had the privilege of belonging to such an outstanding squadron.

Air Vice-Marshal
A. F. C. Hunter C.B.E., A.F.C., D.L.
Honorary Air Commodore
No. 609 (West Riding) Squadron
Royal Auxiliary Air Force, 2006

INTRODUCTION

The Battle of Britain has for long been the centre-point of British historical memory of the Second World War. Historians will argue about its real significance or the relative merits of the Air Force or the Navy as a deterrent, but the one thing that was avoided successfully in 1940 was German invasion. Like the fate of the Spanish Armada in 1588 — another date that used to stick in every schoolchild's memory — the failure of the German Air Force did not make Britain's enemy a great deal weaker, but it did prevent violation of the homeland.

The Battle of Britain was one of the few military campaigns that Britain was prepared for in 1940. Throughout the pre-war years money was spent on creating a defensive shield of modern fighter aircraft, radar stations, ground observers and civil defence measures as a top priority. Perhaps Hitler and the German military leadership judged Britain by the small size and modest performance of the Army and Air Force in the Battle of France; what the enemy failed to grasp was the nature of the complex air defence scheme that was designed to prevent not invasion, but the relentless and ruthless bombing of the British mainland.

It is this scheme that lies at the heart of *Spitfire Pilot*. This account of the Battle of Britain could only have appeared with the blessing of the Air Ministry. Its story reflects quite closely the brief history of the Battle published by the Ministry in March 1941. The various phases of the Battle are clear to see — the early probing attacks by the Luftwaffe during which British pilots learned some hard tactical lessons; the more serious assault in August when ports, military installations and airfields were systematically attacked; the city bombing attacks of September when the German Air Force began at last to take heavy losses; and finally the tail-end of the Battle when the German Air Force tried to lure up British fighters to join in small fighter-to-fighter engagements and instead found themselves experiencing unacceptable rates of attrition. Though these stages were only dimly evident to the pilots who fought a continuous battle from June to October, each marked a definite change in the operational or tactical experience of both sides.

British pilots survived the later phases better as they gained confidence and experience; in the first German attacks in June and July, small in scale compared with the main battle a month later, Crook's squadron took high casualties. By the end of the Battle losses were the exception rather than the rule. Slowly the Few, made famous in Churchill's Commons speech on 20th August 1940, became the Many. Fighter Command ended the battle with more aircraft and pilots than it had begun with thanks to a well-organised training programme and frantic efforts to squeeze Spitfires and Hurricanes out of the aircraft industry. On the other side fighter pilots became a scarcer commodity. The diary entries reveal not just the growing expertise of

British air crew but the relative decline of German pilot performance from the high standards of the cohort that began the battle.

The bare facts and figures, however, say little about what it was like, day in, day out, to fly into combat against an unpredictable and courageous enemy. The diary reveals that for many young men in the late 1930s and early 1940s flying was what they desperately wanted to do. There is not much here about the nature of the war for democracy or the German enemy (throughout referred to as Huns, as they had been during the First World War). Only the Polish pilots who joined the squadron seem to have really hated the Germans because of the destruction of their country in September 1939.

For the young men who fought, the battle was expressed in the language of the school playing field. The sporting metaphors were uniquely English. Who else could write that waiting to shoot down the squadron's one hundredth aircraft was like a batsman poised expectantly at the crease on 99, waiting for the elusive but well-earned century? Whatever efforts might be made now to show that the Battle of Britain is part myth, part truth, the diary of this particular pilot shows beyond doubt that the traditional image of the youthful, fearless and intrepid pilot is really how it was.

Richard Overy
2006

AUGUST 1939–JULY 1940

For our annual camp in August 1939, 609 Squadron went to Church Fenton near Tadcaster.

We were one of the Auxiliary Air Force squadrons (really the R.A.F. equivalent of the Territorial Army), and we did our peace-time training at week-ends and in the evenings during the week. This meant that we had to give up almost all our normal pursuits and spare-time pleasures in the twelve months preceding the war, because training was intensified so much as a result of the international situation that it seemed only just possible to find time to carry on one's normal civilian job, and in addition, to do the flying and ground training in the squadron.

Tennis, golf, rugger, going away for week-ends — we had to cut these out almost entirely and concentrate instead on loops and rolls, formation flying and fighter tactics, armament and engines. But everybody was extraordinarily keen, from the C.O. down to the ground crews, and we all realized the urgency of the situation and the great part that fighter squadrons would play in the event of war. Also, I think that to most of us flying was the dominating interest in our lives — I know that

1

it has always been so to me — and therefore the more flying we did, the better we were pleased.

The experience we gained stood us in good stead in the future, and when the war came, and our training was put to the sternest tests of all, 609 and the other Auxiliary squadrons came through with flying colours and a record which equalled that of the very best regular squadrons.

Summer camp was always good fun. Grand flying in glorious weather, basking lazily in the sun between flights, all packing into cars in the evening and racing into Tadcaster or York, pleasant friends and lively company — what more could anyone ask of life? Altogether we had an enjoyable, if somewhat hardworking, fortnight.

We flew back to Yeadon on Sunday afternoon, 18th August. Exactly a year later to the day we were to have our most successful action of the war and shoot down thirteen German machines in four minutes. But we could not know this at the time and in any case only three of the original members of the squadron were left with us to take part in this action.

For the rest of August the possibility of war steadily increased as the days went by, and I got more and more worried about our wedding, which was to take place on 2nd September. Finally, after some hurried telephoning to Dorothy, who was then in Kent, we decided to bring forward the date to 23rd August. So she came up from London that day, we were married by special licence, and hastily departed on our honeymoon, feeling all the time that Fate might overtake us at any moment.

Next morning the maid came into our room about 8 a.m. and said that I was wanted on the telephone. I had an awful feeling that I knew what it was, and went downstairs with a sinking heart.

I was quite right. It was Paul ringing up to say that five minutes after we left Glenwood the previous evening, the adjutant had rung up to say that mobilization of the Auxiliary Air Force had been ordered. Father spoke to him, and finally got permission for me to return the following day.

So that was that. We had breakfast, read a very gloomy newspaper, and departed. It was a perfect morning, the Lakes were looking as lovely as I have ever seen them, and the prospect of leaving this heavenly spot and finishing our honeymoon, and then going back to war was just too awful for words. Altogether, Thursday, 24th August, ranks as one of the blackest days of my life! We got back for lunch and found that the Territorials had also been mobilized. Paul and I got out our uniforms, packed our kit, and said good-bye.

Ten days later we were at war.

A few days before the declaration of war, 609 Squadron had moved north to its war station, but several of us stayed at Yeadon, as we had not yet completed our training.

We spent a gay month. There was no flying to be done, but we played a lot of rugger and also had some games of mixed hockey with the W.A.A.F.s. These games were amusing but not very skilful, as the W.A.A.F.s were generally chosen for their decorative rather than their athletic qualifications, and the two did not seem to combine very well. We went over to some good parties in Harrogate, and altogether it was probably a very good thing for our immortal souls that on 7th October Patrick, Gordon, Michael, and I were sent down to a Flying Training School in Gloucestershire to join the first war course there.

We arrived a day early, and so there was little to do. We just wandered round rather aimlessly and felt forlorn and depressed. After the good companionship and friendly atmosphere of an Auxiliary squadron, this place felt aloof and unfriendly.

Two days later we felt even more disillusioned. The Auxiliary Air Force always considered itself rather a thing apart from the R.A.F., both as regards discipline and a number of other matters. Nobody had ever suggested to us that this was not the case, and when about nine Auxiliary officers arrived at the school on the first war course and we discovered that we were expected to conform with regular R.A.F. standards of discipline, we felt rather bitter about it.

Actually it was an excellent lesson for our rather conceited selves. I can see that now, but rather failed to perceive it then. Certainly some of the rules were framed to meet the case of boys eighteen to twenty years old straight from school, and we found all this rather childish and said so.

But on the whole, we had the good sense to lie low for a while and not make a nuisance of ourselves.

On our third morning there the whole course was paraded and drilled by Warrant Officer M., a man of

4

fearsome aspect who had been in the Indian Army for twenty-five years.

He told us exactly the poor opinion he had formed of us, our appearance and general smartness, and finally bade us get our hair cut before coming on parade again.

We were all very indignant — being told to have a hair-cut by an N.C.O. — incredible impudence! We certainly weren't going to do anything of the sort, etc., etc. Anyway, that evening a slightly embarrassed party went down to the little barber's shop in the village and all emerged later with a truly convict crop. (I have already remarked that Warrant Officer M. was a very formidable-looking man!) We paraded next morning all shaven and shorn — except Peter. He swore that he always wore his hair pretty long and certainly wasn't going to part with it for anything. A very impressive storm of anger broke over his well-covered head, but he said nothing and finally the storm subsided. We felt that perhaps the honours were even in this first encounter.

However, we soon found life more bearable. By working hard and doing better than any previous course at the school, we created a fairly good impression and finally the authorities (and even our old adversary, Warrant Officer M.) seemed to realize that we were really keen to do well, and they became much more friendly and human in their attitude.

For the first two months at F.T.S. we worked very hard indeed, both at flying and ground work. Parade was at 7.45 a.m., and after that we flew all morning and had lectures all afternoon, and on alternate days lectures in the morning and flying in the afternoon.

I enjoyed the flying very much and did not have any trouble with this, but the lectures were not so enjoyable.

To have to sit at a desk with books in front of you and see an instructor explaining a navigational problem on the blackboard is far too like algebra lessons at school for my liking. But I think we all realized that this might prove very useful and even essential to us one day in the not-so-distant future, and so we worked hard and didn't go to sleep and waded through engines and supercharging, airframes and navigation till we possessed a fairly good knowledge of these subjects.

At Flying Training School the Chief Ground Instructor is really the equivalent of the housemaster at a public school. He watches your progress, punishes you if you are lazy, gives you leave or stops it as you deserve, and altogether keeps you up to scratch.

We had an excellent C.G.I. and after a somewhat austere welcome, we got on well with him. He was "a beast but a just beast", and if you went to him with a good case he was always reasonable.

In his more humorous moments (such as guest nights) he used to refer to himself as "the old bastard". He was in his office one day when he heard somebody outside in the passage say to someone else "Is the old bastard in?" This amused him greatly!

We also had an excellent Chief Flying Instructor, Squadron Leader O. He had spent a lot of time on flying-boats out in Singapore and had met Gordon out there. He was a grand person, very powerfully built and with a striking face that might have been good-looking but for a somewhat battered nose, the result of a lot of boxing. He had a terrific personality and if he made us work like niggers, at any rate he got the best out of us.

Not long after we left F.T.S. he got married and shortly after he went to command a Hurricane squadron, and was killed in August during a German attack on an aerodrome. We were very shocked to hear of his death; he always seemed so alive and tough that it was difficult to imagine him dying.

I enjoyed the flying and soon got to like the Harvard. This machine is one of the types that we are getting from America and I must say that it gave me a very good impression of American aircraft.

At first it had rather a bad reputation in the R.A.F. because a number of fatal crashes occurred, some of them involving very experienced pilots.

Certainly the Harvard does require handling with care, and possesses a very vicious spin, especially to the right. But if you treat them with a little respect, then they are pleasant machines, and we became devoted to them.

I remember that I was impressed by my first spin in a Harvard. At about 6,000 feet I throttled back and when she had almost stalled, I put on right rudder. The machine promptly executed a fearsome leap over to the right and started to spin down very rapidly. I didn't wait very long before recovering; I put on full left rudder and pushed the control column forward to the dashboard. She stopped spinning almost immediately,

7

but I had the stick too far forward and the result was that we came out in a dive beyond the vertical.

We lost at least 3,000 feet before pulling up, and I had considerable respect for a Harvard spin after that.

She was also very different from a Hind for loops and other aerobatics. On my first attempt at a loop I climbed up to a good height, then dived to about 220 m.p.h. and started to pull up. I got the stick farther and farther back, till, on top of the loop, it was right in my tummy just as though I was flying a Hind.

The Harvard immediately did an incredibly rapid flick roll and I found myself right way up again, feeling puzzled and a little breathless.

I tried again, with precisely the same result, and then after about five minutes' experimenting I discovered that it was all very easy if only I got the stick back much more slowly. But I still used to do inadvertent flick rolls now and again.

In November we had our first taste of night flying. Personally, I had been rather looking forward to it, but as the day approached there seemed to be no lack of helpful friends who explained at great length the hazards and difficulties involved.

The chosen night happened to be as black as ink, so dark that it was quite impossible to distinguish between ground and sky, and in a somewhat resigned mood I taxied out on to the flare path with my instructor.

"O.K.," he shouted cheerfully, "you've got her. Away you go."

8

I opened up the throttle and we tore along the line of flares, doing a magnificent swerve which he promptly corrected by a vicious kick on the rudder bar.

We roared over the last flare and suddenly went off into complete darkness. The contrast between this and the flare path was so sharp and so quick that it hit me almost like a blow in the face. I almost panicked, but just managed to remember the instructions that had been drilled into me, "Watch your instruments and *don't* try to look out". So I glued my eyes on to the dashboard, and concentrated on the artificial horizon till my eyes almost popped out of my head. Undercarriage up, airscrew into coarse pitch, speed 120 m.p.h., and the Sperry horizon still level. I climbed up to 600 feet and did a gentle climbing turn to the left, still flying entirely on instruments. Very slowly over my left shoulder the twinkling lights of the flare path came into view. They looked very real and friendly; I felt they were the only things in the world upon which I could really count at that moment.

I started to Morse our identification letter on the signalling lamp, and a second later an answering green light flashed out of the darkness, winked several times at us, and vanished. O.K., we have permission to land. I turned across wind and put the undercarriage down, fine pitch, flaps down, trim back, and then peered into the darkness as we slid gently down towards the lights at 75 m.p.h. They seemed to be coming up at us very slowly. It was a lovely sensation gliding down through the still night air and I was so fascinated that I was rather taken by surprise at the speed with which we dropped the last 200 feet. "Look out," said a warning voice from the rear cockpit, "we're nearly down." I still couldn't see the ground, though it was obvious from the line of flares that we were only a few feet up.

We hit it quite suddenly, rather before I had expected, and bounced up again. I was so surprised that I just sat there and waited. There was a grunt over the inter-com. and my guardian angel banged open the throttle and lowered us on to the ground again, rather more gently this time. We taxied quickly off the flare path and stopped.

"Well, how do you like it?" I replied that it didn't seem too bad, which was a thumping lie actually, because I didn't see how I could ever go through this performance solo.

But we did another forty-five minutes of it; I was then tested by the C.F.I., who took a very poor view of my first landing, and then after a couple more he let me go solo.

I managed to get round without doing anything very drastic, and then walked over to the crew room, feeling distinctly proud of myself. Everybody else had gone solo too; there had been no mishaps at all, and we all decided that it had been rather good fun.

I suddenly realized that I was more tired than I had been for years. It is rather a mental strain, the first time. And so to bed about 4.30 a.m. and a long sleep till lunch.

At the beginning of December we received a curt intimation that we should soon be called upon to face our "Wings" exam. We took the threat seriously and worked like niggers, and even one or two blithe spirits who had never done a hard day's work in their lives could now be seen doing at least half an hour's revision every evening.

The thought of failure was too awful to contemplate. Our wingless uniforms gave us such an inferiority complex that in hotels or any other public place we used to shiver ostentatiously and keep muffled up in greatcoats, thus hiding our shame from the world; which probably didn't care a damn anyway.

As the ordeal approached, we viewed our prospects with misgivings, but it was all right on the day and we all passed. Rarely have I felt such satisfaction as when Dorothy sewed that coveted badge on my tunic. A number of people came down to the New Inn that night to celebrate; D. sewed on several pairs of wings for them, and we had an amusing dinner party in honour of the great event.

We were now real pilots! On looking back now I think we all realize that we didn't know very much about service flying, at any rate compared with what we have learnt since, but we all felt very important at the time.

The winter of 1939–40 was an appalling one, and as the weather got worse the aerodrome became more and more muddy, till finally all flying was stopped, and this meant that life became very dull. However, we used to have some cheery evenings at the New Inn, and often Michael and Gordon and the others came down and had dinner with us, and stayed afterwards in the little bar, which filled up more and more as the evening progressed, till finally you could scarcely move and the atmosphere was so thick with smoke that it looked like a fog.

Towards the end of January the weather improved and we started flying over at another aerodrome near Oxford, our own aerodrome being still a sea of mud. We were now in the Advanced Training Squadron and the flying was good fun.

Our new Flight Commander was "Roger"; he was a grand instructor and a most amusing and entertaining person. We got on very well with him. We used to work a lot in pairs (Gordon being my partner), and went off on navigation or reconnaissance exercises over a large area of southern England. We also did a lot of formation flying and camera gun work. Sometimes two or three of us would meet at some pre-arranged rendezvous, and then go low flying all over the high ground above the village. (I hasten to add that this was the authorized low flying area!)

We used to roar down the roads just over charabancs and cars and then, climbing up again, go back to Oxford, rolling and diving and generally playing the fool all the way. Those were very happy days and we were very happy and light-hearted and carefree. Flying seemed to be the only thing in the world that really mattered, and we were so absorbed in it that it seemed to dominate our whole conversation and outlook.

My chief delight was always aerobatics. I used to spend hour after hour practising loops and rolls above a railway line so that I could tell if I was coming out straight or not. When I had mastered these, I did half rolls off the top, and then, best and most exhilarating of them all, upward rolls, till finally I felt that I could handle a Harvard with confidence in any position which I (or the aircraft) chose to assume.

I think almost the chief joy of doing aerobatics in a fast machine is the sense of understanding which gradually develops between you and the aeroplane, so that eventually you no longer feel that you are a separate being, but rather that you are just a part of this superb piece of machinery which races so effortlessly through the skies at your command.

Aerobatics may not enter much into modern air fighting, but the ability to recover from any position in the air, instantaneously and without even thinking about it, is of enormous value in a scrap where there are so many other things upon which one has to concentrate, and when the pilot's handling of the aircraft must be absolutely automatic.

I possess now a great admiration for the flying training given to pilots by the R.A.F. I don't think there is any training system in the world to touch it for thoroughness, and it also seems to impart to many of the pupils those qualities of initiative and dash which we seem to produce to our great advantage over the German Air Force, who are not half such good individualists. Certainly when we left F.T.S. to take our own parts in the war we possessed a sound background of flying knowledge and experience, even though we still had a great deal to learn.

By 4th April we had completed all our flying, both day and night, and so we got a few days' leave before going to practice camp to do our air firing. This proved to be a grand ending to the course; the weather was good on the whole; we did a lot of flying and firing and had some very good parties in the evening. The fortnight finished all too soon and we returned to Gloucestershire.

Our time at F.T.S. was now almost over and little remained to be done except to pack our kit, bid farewell to everybody, and, almost more important than anything else, hear what squadrons we were posted to. All the Auxiliary officers had applied to return to their old squadrons, but we were rather anxious about this and thought that we might be posted to some unspeakable job, such as Army Co-operation or day bombers. But when the postings came through they pleased almost everybody, and Michael, Gordon, and I were all returned to 609, to our intense relief.

Our last night in the mess was a gay one, and (as Mr. Churchill once put it), the use of alcohol was not excluded. The Group Captain, who was in fighting form, made a long speech and assured us that we should teach "that damned Austrian house painter" a good lesson.

He also paid our course several compliments, which I think were quite well deserved on the whole. We had worked hard and done our best, and our results, and particularly the air firing results, were the best ever obtained at the school.

I hated the thought of saying good-bye to everybody. There were fifteen officers on our course, and we had spent the whole winter together and got to know each other very well indeed. With all the monotony and boredom that we had to put up with sometimes, quite a lot of friction and bad temper might have been expected. But it never materialized, and one could not have wished for pleasanter or more entertaining company. They were a grand crowd.

There were several South Africans who had been in the Cambridge or London University Air Squadrons; Claude and Ian were two of these, and were in the Fighter Flight, while the other two, Hugh and Tony, were in the Bomber Flight.

Ian went to 610 Fighter Squadron, while poor old Claude, who was a magnificent pilot and had absolutely set his heart on getting to a Fighter Squadron also, was sent instead to an Army Co-operation Squadron. This made him very miserable, and for some time after we left F.T.S. we used to write to each other in an attempt to get him posted to 609 with us. But it was no good. Later in the summer, however, he achieved his ambition and got a transfer to fighters. He was delighted.

A month or two later his machine was badly hit during a fight, and though he managed to land it, he died of wounds soon afterwards.

Hugh and Tony both went to Blenheims in Coastal Command. Hugh was posted "missing" after a patrol over the Channel in August, while Tony fought all during the summer and winter of 1940, made very many raids, and got the D.F.C., and was then killed in the spring of 1941.

15

"Farmer Bill" also went to Blenheims in Coastal Command and was killed in the autumn of 1940. He was a farmer in Wiltshire, and I remember a silly story of his, how his horse often used to come into the farm, and how surprised visitors were upon arrival to see a horse staring at them from the dining-room window.

Patrick, who had been in 609 with us, decided to change to bombers and went to the same squadron as Tony. I haven't heard from him for some time, but he is still alive and kicking, and has just got the D.F.C.

Greg was posted with Claude to Army Co-operation, and this almost broke his heart. He tried for many months to get out, but did not succeed.

However, in the end he got the long-awaited transfer, and went to a Hurricane squadron. I met him just before this, and he was delighted about his good luck. It was grand to see him again.

I heard from him shortly after, when he seemed to be enjoying life, and then I suddenly saw his name in a casualty list, missing, believed killed in action. It seemed so ironical that both he and Claude should move heaven and earth to get posted to fighters, and then be killed almost immediately their great ambition was fulfilled.

Then there was Basil, very quiet, and with a slow delightful smile that was one of the most engaging things I ever saw. He was a marvellous squash player and one time Eton cricket captain. He was posted to 111 Squadron; like the rest of us he had set his heart on getting to a fighter squadron. He was killed in one of the battles on the south coast in August.

John, Julian, and Peter were all in 601 Squadron, and we saw a lot of the first two at F.T.S., as they used to come down to the New Inn with Gordon and Michael. John was an exceptionally good pilot, and I don't think any of us were surprised when he got the D.F.C. in August. Julian was killed in one of the big battles off the Isle of Wight in August. He was a delightful person, and we were all very shocked to hear of his death.

And then there were Bunny and Louise, who used to live with us at the New Inn, and who were always such good fun.

So much more could be written about them all and the grand times that we used to have together, but it would take too long.

So Dorothy and I said good-bye to everybody, and drove off on our way north.

Within a few months, out of these fifteen friends, five had got the D.F.C., and eight, alas, were dead.

It was grand to be home again, and we spent a pleasant week's leave before joining the squadron in Scotland.

On Saturday morning, 4th May, I said good-bye at home and drove off; not without a certain feeling of importance, on active service for the first time.

I had arranged to go north with Gordon and Michael, and so we met at the Queens in Leeds and had lunch with Pip, who was down on leave. He was B Flight Commander and he told us that we were all going into his flight; we were very pleased in consequence and celebrated our new partnership in several rounds of rye and dry, after which lunch proved to be a very hilarious meal.

Michael and I left in the Wolseley after lunch and started on our long journey north. It was a perfect spring day, and the countryside seemed alive with warmth and colour as we drove gaily up the Great North Road, through Newcastle and on to Alnwick, where we stopped for dinner. On again through Berwick-on-Tweed, and then some distance farther on we turned off to the right, climbed up over the hill, and saw the aerodrome down on the other side, with the sea beyond.

It was good to be back with the squadron again after such a long absence. They had had a very quiet and on the whole dull winter, and had only been in action once when a solitary Heinkel was shot down by Desmond after it had tried to attack a convoy. We had suffered no losses at all since the outbreak of war and everybody was in good form and enjoying life to the utmost.

Certainly it was a pleasant spot. There was plenty of golf and squash and tennis; the war was quiet and hardly entered into the scheme of things, and we could go into Edinburgh on most evenings. Altogether it was an enjoyable and easy existence.

The next day I did my first trip in a Spitfire. I had waited for this moment for nearly two years, and when it came it was just as exciting as I had always expected.

Having mastered the cockpit drill, I got in and taxied out on the aerodrome, sat there for one moment to check that everything was O.K., and then opened up to full throttle. The effect took my breath away. The engine opened up with a great smooth roar, the Spitfire leapt forward like a bullet and tore madly across the aerodrome, and before I had realized quite what had happened I was in the air. I felt as though the machine was completely out of control and running away with me. However, I collected my scattered wits, raised the undercarriage, and put the airscrew into coarse pitch, and then looked round for the aerodrome, which to my astonishment I saw was already miles behind.

After a few minutes' cruising round I realized that this fearsome beast was perhaps not quite so formidable as I had thought in that first breathless minute, so I decided to try a landing. This came off reasonably satisfactorily, and I took off again, feeling much more sure of myself. So I climbed up to a good height and played about in the clouds in this superb new toy and did a few gentle dives to 400 m.p.h., which gave me a tremendous thrill. Altogether I was almost light-headed with exhilaration when I landed at the end of an hour's flight, and I felt that I could ask nothing more of life.

Actually, once you have done a few hours' flying in a Spitfire and become accustomed to the great power and speed, then it is an extraordinarily easy machine to fly and it is absolutely marvellous for aerobatics. Practically everybody who has flown a Spitfire thinks it is the most marvellous aircraft ever built, and I am no exception to the general rule. I grew to like it more than any other machine I have flown. It is so small and compact and neat, yet it possesses devastating fire power, and it is still probably the best and the fastest fighter in the world. The new fighters which will soon be coming into service will have to do very well to equal the Spitfire's amazing record of success.

I thoroughly enjoyed my first week with the squadron, and came to the conclusion that if this was the life of the average fighter pilot in war, then I didn't mind how long the war continued. I played some squash with Gordon and Michael, and we did one or two hours' practice flying every day, and soon felt quite at home in the Spitfire.

On Thursday, 9th May, we had the day off; and so the three of us went into Edinburgh and had a grand evening, starting with dinner, and then going on to a variety show at the Empire. The house was packed with a noisy and appreciative audience, and there was an amusing episode when a rather boozed sailor climbed up on to the front of the stage and tried to dance. He was cheered wildly, and then the side curtains were quickly drawn across and exactly three seconds later when they were drawn back again the sailor had been spirited away. We all cheered more than ever.

The following morning my batman came in and woke me with the words, "Jerry's into Holland and Belgium." I bounded out of bed — this was astonishing news. At breakfast everybody else seemed to be equally staggered, but behind the surprise I think there was a general sense of relief that the war had now really "started", and that as a result we might soon see some action. Now we could give the Huns a taste of their own medicine! Thus we thought, in our ignorance and complacency.

However, the new offensive did not disturb immediately our easy ways of life, and I think the only result was that we cancelled a cocktail party which was to have been held the following week. There was no bombing and no enemy activity, though it seemed certain that we should soon be moved south.

But apparently Fate had other plans for me, because two days later I jumped gaily out of bed and in doing so I tore the ligament in my left knee; it had given me trouble for years as the result of a ski-ing accident. The doctor did what he could, but it was still hopeless, and the following day I was sent down to Peebles Hydro for an operation.

A few days later Dorothy came down from Gullane to join me, and she brought the news that the squadron had just moved down to Northolt. Obviously the long-awaited day of action was approaching, and I cursed bitterly the fate that kept me in bed at such a time. Day after day, while my leg was recovering, we sat on the balcony in glorious weather and listened to the wireless as it announced the increasingly grave news from France.

While we were having such an easy and pleasant life, 609 were going into action for the first time at Dunkirk, and also having our first losses.

On 30th, 31st May, and 1st June, the squadron did patrols over Dunkirk to cover the evacuation of troops from the beaches.

We shot a number of Huns down and lost four of our pilots. Desmond was also killed near Frinton-on-Sea;

he lost his way back in bad weather and ran out of petrol, and was killed in trying to make a forced landing.

I think there is no doubt that some of these losses were due to inexperience and lack of caution. None of us had ever been in action before, and everybody's idea was to go all out for the first Hun that appeared.

This policy does not pay when you are fighting a cunning and crafty foe, and the Germans frequently used to send over a decoy aircraft with a number of fighters hovering in the sun some thousands of feet above, who would come down like a ton of bricks on anybody attacking the decoy. This ruse almost certainly accounted for one pilot, Presser, and possibly one or two others — the last that anybody saw of Presser was when he was diving down to attack a Junkers 88, and there were definitely some Messerschmidts above.

My knee was now improving rapidly, and on 16th June Dorothy and I left Peebles. We returned home and spent a few days in the Lakes, and on 29th June we departed for London. I said good-bye to Dorothy at Marylebone and went out to Northolt, to start the most exciting and eventful time of my life.

A great change had come over the squadron since I had left them only seven weeks before. We had a new C.O. and there were several new pilots to replace the Dunkirk losses.

The old easy-going outlook on life had vanished, and everybody now seemed to realize that war was not the fairly pleasant affair that it had always seemed hitherto.

Altogether the general mood now appeared to be one of rather grim determination.

My first two days at Northolt were spent mainly in practice flying, and I soon felt quite at home in the Spitfire again.

On the Monday evening, 1st July, I came down into the anteroom, just after dinner, and found Pip gathering everybody together, as an order had just come through that twelve of us were to do a reconnaissance of some aerodromes in northern France the following morning, in order to see what machines the enemy was assembling there. If our patrols reported a good concentration at any aerodrome then bombers would be dispatched immediately to beat the place up.

I don't think anybody was particularly enthusiastic about the idea, but anyway it had to be done, so we got out maps and discussed the route: down to Hawkinge (Folkestone) at dawn to refuel and get breakfast, then straight over to Boulogne, along the coast to the mouth of the Somme, and then turn in to Abbeville to inspect the aerodrome there. After this we should turn south-west again to Rouen, inspect the aerodrome, and turn north towards the coast, crossing it at Dieppe and having a look at that aerodrome also. We reckoned that we should get to Abbeville easily, but that we might expect a lot of trouble any time after that.

And so to bed to get what sleep we could. I gathered afterwards that nobody slept well, and I certainly didn't. I had never seen the enemy before, and I kept wondering what it would be like to go into action for the first time.

We got up about 3.30a.m. It was a lovely morning and we got into cars and went down to the point where our machines were already being run up. I checked up everything in the cockpit particularly carefully, and a few minutes later we took off and headed south-east, down through Kent to Folkestone. It was the first time I had flown with the whole squadron, and it was certainly a rather inspiring sight to see eleven other Spitfires all thundering on together.

We landed at Hawkinge, and the ground crews immediately started to refuel the aircraft. We stood around and smoked cigarettes incessantly and made some rather forced conversation, and suffered from that unpleasant empty feeling in the tummy that one always experiences at such moments.

Altogether a very good specimen of squadron "wind up"!

So many recollections come back to me at such moments. I thought of a summer's evening two years before, when Glen had been at camp here and I had come down to see him. How different it had all seemed then.

I thought of those grand July week-ends that we had spent at Brenley, only a few miles away, and most of all I thought of those occasions when we had sailed from Folkestone *en route* for Boulogne and Switzerland. I had a feeling that I wasn't going to enjoy this cross-Channel trip quite as much as those previous ones!

The machines were now refuelled and we climbed in, started the engines, and taxied out to take off. A few moments later we were in the air. We made one circuit of Folkestone, and then headed straight out for the French coast. But an anti-climax was in store for us. As we approached France we could see a ground mist covering the countryside, and the ground itself was invisible. This was no good, so we turned about and landed at Hawkinge with our task still unexecuted.

We spent an unpleasant day at Hawkinge, and although somebody went over to have a look at the weather at lunch-time, it was still too misty.

During the afternoon instructions came through that one machine was to go over at 6p.m., and if the weather was suitable, we would take off at 7p.m. Our scout returned at about 6.45p.m. with the news that the weather was now O.K. The time had arrived. I really didn't care very much any longer; after waiting all day I was so fed up that it was a relief to get going and try to get it done this time at any rate.

We took off again, and, having circled Folkestone, we steered out towards Boulogne. The C.O. was flying below with two other machines in order to do the actual "spotting", while the other nine machines flew above and behind to guard him and look out for enemy fighters.

In a matter of four or five minutes I saw Boulogne ahead and we turned right and flew down the coast to the mouth of the Somme, where we turned inland towards Abbeville and started to dive at very high speed. As we approached the aerodrome, an accurate burst of A.A. fire appeared just in front of us, and I swerved to the right and climbed slightly. We soon passed out of range of the battery, and, the C.O. having inspected Abbeville, turned right for Rouen. From now onwards we could expect enemy fighters, and we scanned the sky anxiously, looking above and behind us almost the whole time. But none appeared, and soon I could see the Seine ahead, winding down to the coast in great S bends.

Only a few weeks before, the bitterest fighting of the war had taken place in the countryside below us and along the banks of the Seine. But it all looked very peaceful that evening, and travelling at the height and great speed that we were going, I could see no signs of the great struggle that had just finished.

We flew over Rouen aerodrome and then turned north for Dieppe and the coast. We were on the last lap now. The coast loomed up ahead and a moment later I gave a sigh of relief as we left French soil behind us. But our troubles were not quite over, for after we were a mile or so from the coast, another accurate burst of A.A. fire came up from a flak ship anchored off Dieppe. This burst came up just ahead of us and rocked several machines violently, though no damage was done.

Shortly afterwards we crossed the English coast at Dungeness, and turned up towards Folkestone. Gosh, it was good to be back!

When we landed we found that the cook had gone, so had to cook ourselves some eggs and bacon. But we just didn't care a hang about anything, and sat and ate our meal and felt jolly glad to have got the job over at last!

★   ★   ★

Our stay at Northolt was now almost up because on Thursday morning, 4th July, the enemy bombed Portland, and so orders came through later in the morning that 609 were to move to the south-west as reinforcements.

The squadron accordingly moved down on the Thursday afternoon, but I stayed behind, as it was my day off, and I had to have another medical board about my knee to see that it was now O.K. So I spent the night at Hampstead with Dorothy and turned up at Kingsway the following morning.

I was prodded and pushed and altogether thoroughly "vetted" and pronounced A.1., though the doctor was a bit annoyed to find that I had already been flying, as the last medical board at Peebles had passed me as unfit for flying till my knee was examined again. However, he soon calmed down.

So I went out to Northolt again, and flew down that evening.

We were the only squadron in that sector at the time, and so we had to get up at 3.30a.m. and went to bed again at about 11.30p.m. — altogether a pretty long day.

We had a number of alarms and went out over the sea as hard as we could, hoping to see some enemy, but I think most of these scares were quite without foundation, and after a day or so I came to the conclusion that I might spend months at this game and never see any action. How little I knew!

A few days later we moved to a new aerodrome near Salisbury. This is a very good strategic base for the defence both of Southampton and Portland, and it was to be our home for some time to come.

We continued, however, to use the advanced base and we flew down at dawn every day and returned home at dusk.

I was sharing a room with Peter, and we rose as usual on the Tuesday morning, 9th July, and had early breakfast at 4.30 a.m., and then flew down to our advanced base in bad weather.

At about 9 a.m. a report came through that a German machine was attacking ships off the coast, so Peter and I took off to investigate. The clouds were so low that they were actually covering the hills between us and the sea, but we found a gap just where the road runs through a little valley. We roared through this gap just above the road (we heard later that two cyclists were so alarmed by these two Spitfires racing through just above their heads, that they threw themselves into the ditch), and then found ourselves over the coast. But it was a false alarm, and so, rather disappointed, we turned back to the aerodrome.

We sat in the tent again and listened to the rain dripping steadily outside, and Peter and I fixed to go up to London together on the following day in his car, as we both had the day off, and he was going up to see his wife.

At about 6.30 p.m. we were ordered to patrol Weymouth, and so Peter, Michael, and I took off, Peter leading.

We circled round for about three-quarters of an hour, and saw nothing at all. Peter was getting very fed up with this apparently unnecessary flying, and we circled round the aerodrome and asked permission to land. We were told, however, to continue our patrol and turned out again over Weymouth at about 7,000 feet. A moment later, looking out towards the left, I saw an aircraft dive into a layer of cloud about two miles away and then reappear. I immediately called up Peter on the R.T., and he swung us into line astern, and turned left towards the enemy.

A moment later I saw one or two more Huns appear, and recognized them as Junkers 87 dive-bombers. I immediately turned on my reflector sights, put my gun button on to "fire" and settled down to enjoy a little slaughter of a few Ju. 87s, as they are rather helpless machines.

I was flying last on the line, and we were now travelling at high speed and rapidly approaching the enemy, when I happened to look round behind. To my intense surprise and dismay, I saw at least nine Messerschmidt 110s about 2,000 feet above us. They were just starting to dive on us when I saw them, and as they were diving they were overtaking us rapidly.

This completely altered the situation. We were now hopelessly outnumbered, and in a very dangerous position, and altogether I began to see that if we were not jolly quick we should all be dead in a few seconds.

I immediately called up Peter and Michael and shouted desperately, "Look out behind, Messerschmidts behind" — all the time looking over my shoulder at the leading enemy fighter, who was now almost in range.

But though I kept shouting, both Peter and Michael continued straight on at the bombers ahead, and they were now almost in range and about to open fire.

I have never felt so desperate or so helpless in my life, as when, in spite of my warnings, these two flew steadily on, apparently quite oblivious of the fact that they were going to be struck down from the rear in a few seconds.

At that moment the leading Messerschmidt opened fire at me and I saw his shells and tracer bullets going past just above my head. They were jolly close too. I immediately did a very violent turn to the left and dived through a layer of cloud just below.

I emerged from the cloud going at very high speed — probably over 400 mph., and saw a Ju. 87 just ahead of me. I opened fire (my first real shot of the war), and he seemed to fly right through my tracer bullets, but when I turned round to follow him, he had disappeared.

I then climbed up into the cloud again to try to rejoin the others. I saw an Me. 110 some distance above me, and I pulled up into a steep climb and fired at him but without result. He turned away immediately, and I lost him.

At that moment I saw dimly a machine moving in the cloud on my left and flying parallel to me. I stalked him through the cloud, and when he emerged into a patch of clear sky I saw that it was a Ju. 87.

I was in an ideal position to attack and opened fire and put the remainder of my ammunition — about 2,000 rounds — into him at very close range. Even in the heat of the moment I well remember my amazement at the shattering effect of my fire. Pieces flew off his fuselage and cockpit covering, a stream of smoke appeared from the engine, and a moment later a great sheet of flame licked out from the engine cowling and he dived down vertically. The flames enveloped the whole machine and he went straight down, apparently quite slowly, for about five thousand feet, till he was just a shapeless burning mass of wreckage.

Absolutely fascinated by the sight, I followed him down, and saw him hit the sea with a great burst of white foam. He disappeared immediately, and apart from a green patch in the water there was no sign that anything had happened. The crew made no attempt to get out, and they were obviously killed by my first burst of fire.

I had often wondered what would be my feelings when killing somebody like this, and especially when seeing them go down in flames. I was rather surprised to reflect afterwards that my only feeling had been one of considerable elation — and a sort of bewildered surprise because it had all been so easy.

I turned back for the coast, and started to call up Peter and Michael on the R.T. But there was no response, and as far as Peter was concerned, I was already calling to the void.

A moment later I saw another Spitfire flying home on a very erratic course, obviously keeping a very good look behind. I joined up with it, and recognized Michael, and together we bolted for the English coast like a couple of startled rabbits.

I made a perfectly bloody landing on the aerodrome and overshot so badly that I nearly turned the Spitfire on her nose in my efforts to pull up before hitting the hedge. I got out to talk to Michael and found to my surprise that my hand was quite shaky and even my voice was unsteady, due I suppose, to a fairly even mixture of fright, intense excitement, and a sort of reckless exhilaration because I had just been in action for the first time and shot somebody down, and the full significance of that rather startling fact was beginning to dawn on me now that I had time to think.

Michael had left his R.T. in the "transmit" position instead of "receive" and so had not heard my warning shouts at the beginning of the action.

Fortunately for him, however, he turned it over just in time, and heard me say "Messerschmidt". He whipped round and found himself being attacked by three Me. 110s. He had very great difficulty in escaping, got into a spin, recovered and then spun the other way, and came home having fired almost all his rounds at various Me. 110s and Ju. 87s, though without being able to see any results.

He saw a great flurry of machines in the sky about a mile away, which must have been Peter's last effort against an overwhelming number of Messerschmidts. Knowing Peter, I bet he put up a hell of a fight before they got him down.

As soon as our machines were refuelled and rearmed, six of us flew out over the sea to look for him. But there was no sign of him at all, and his body was never recovered.

I think there is no doubt that he also had left his R.T. on "transmit" and so did not hear my warnings, or else perhaps he was thinking that there were only a very few enemy, as we had been told, and therefore the possibility of attack from the rear simply did not occur to him. There had been so many false alarms that he was rather in the frame of mind — "Nothing can ever happen at Weymouth."

We took off just before dusk to return to base. Gordon could not come as his machine had been slightly damaged earlier in the day, and I left him standing outside the tent, looking rather disconsolate because he had not been able to take part in the action with Michael and me. It was the last time I ever saw him.

We got back and I went up to my room in the mess. Everything was just the same as Peter and I had left it only eighteen hours before; his towel was still in the window where he had thrown it during our hurried dressing. But he was dead now. I simply could not get used to such sudden and unexpected death, and there flashed across my mind the arrangements we had made to go up to London together the following day. It all seemed so ironical, so tragic, so futile. I felt that I could not sleep in that room again, and so I took my things and went into Gordon's bed next door and slept there.

But I could not get out of my head the thought of Peter, with whom we had been talking and laughing that day, now lying in the cockpit of his wrecked Spitfire at the bottom of the English Channel.

I felt much better next morning, had a late breakfast, and made out my combat report, and then went into lunch with the others.

In the middle of lunch Pip was called to the telephone, and a few minutes later I went out into the hall and found him standing there looking very worried and unhappy. Peter's wife had just been ringing up, wondering why he had not telephoned her about his trip to London that afternoon. The telegram had not yet reached her, and so Pip had to tell her the news. It all seemed so awful; I was seeing for the first time at very close quarters all the distress and unhappiness that casualties cause. I walked out of the mess and drove to the station, very thankful to be doing something that took my mind on to other subjects. And I never saw Pip again, either.

I met Dorothy in London and we had a pleasant dinner together. She was delighted about my first Hun, though naturally very worried and depressed about the other events. I also rang up home and told the family with considerable pride that I had at last been in action and managed to bag a Hun.

We went out to Hampstead for the night to the flat where D. was staying, and early next morning I went down to Waterloo to catch the train back. I arrived at the aerodrome at lunch time and was walking up the steps of the mess when I met a Squadron Leader who was working in Operations Room. He told me that there had been another fight early that morning and both Pip and Gordon had been killed. The whole squadron was now in the air and apparently a lot of fighting was going on all along the south coast.

I could get no details of what had happened, and I sat alone in the mess all afternoon, feeling more miserable and more stunned than I have ever felt before.

Everybody arrived back after dark, dog-tired and utterly depressed. I shall never forget seeing them all come into the mess — people who, normally, appeared not to have a care in the world just flopped into chairs and sat there and said not a word.

I rang up Dorothy and told her the news, and I think that she was as shocked as I was. She had only met Pip on a few occasions, but knew Gordon very well indeed.

What happened in the morning was this: a ship was being bombed by a large enemy formation south of Portland, and five Spitfires led by Pip took off to go to the spot.

They saw the enemy while they were still some distance away, in the usual German formation with bombers below and fighters guarding them above. The Spitfires were outnumbered by ridiculous odds, but Pip, who had never hesitated for one second at rugger or anything else in his life, did hot hesitate now in this last and greatest moment of all. He detached two machines to try and hold off the enemy fighters (of which there were at least twenty), while he led the other two Spitfires against the enemy bombers below which were attacking the ship.

It was hopeless from the very start. The Messerschmidts dived down on top of our small formation and

35

everybody was separated immediately. Gordon was last seen diving down into the attack and after that nobody saw him again.

After a brief but very sharp fight, during which two enemy dive-bombers were almost definitely destroyed, the enemy formation departed, and Jarvis saw a Spitfire flying back towards the coast, going very slowly and with smoke pouring from it.

This was Pip. A moment later he jumped out, opened his parachute, and dropped into the water. Jarvis circled round him, but Pip gave no sign of recognition, and shortly after, when a boat picked him up, he died as soon as they got him on board. He had been hit twice in the right leg and was also burnt, but it was probably the shock and being for so long in the water that killed him. I think that if he had dropped on land and been attended to quickly he would have lived, because he was incredibly strong and tough.

An immediate search for Gordon was made both by aeroplanes and also naval launches from Portland, but he was not found.

It is difficult to describe my feelings during the next few days. We had lost three pilots in thirty-six hours, all of them in fights in which we had been hopelessly outnumbered, and I felt that there was now really nothing left to care about, because obviously, from the law of probability, one could not expect to survive many more encounters of a similar nature.

When one thinks of the losses sustained in war, particularly by the Army, to lose three people in two days seems very trifling. But in a squadron there are so few pilots, and it really seems more like a rather large family than anything else, and therefore three deaths at once seems very heavy indeed.

Again compared with the experiences of squadrons during the fighting in France, such losses are small, because some squadrons in France were wiped out almost to a man in a few days. But they were taking part in heavy and continuous fighting where one expects losses and also they were destroying very much greater numbers of Germans than they themselves were losing, so they could feel, to put it bluntly, that they were getting value for money, which is a very big factor in maintaining spirits and morale.

But our losses had been sustained in two small encounters, and we had hardly anything to count against it in the way of enemy shot down.

So, quite apart from the death of one's friends, we all felt very depressed, because obviously things weren't going well.

Gordon's death in particular made a deep impression on me, because I knew him much better than I knew Pip. We were at school together, and he, Michael, and I had spent the whole war together, and were so accustomed to being in each other's company that I could not then (and still cannot now) get used to the idea that we should not see Gordon again or spend any more of our gay evenings together or rag him about the moustache of which he was so proud.

He was a delightful person, a very amusing and charming companion, and one of the most generous people I ever knew, both as regards material matters and, more important still, in his outlook and views.

He was also a brilliant athlete, a Cambridge Hockey Blue and Scots International. It always used to delight me to watch Gordon playing any game, whether hockey, tennis, or squash, because he played with such a natural ease and grace — the unmistakable sign of a first-class athlete.

He could not have wished to die in more gallant circumstances.

But if Gordon's death was a greater shock to me personally, Pip's death was a terrible blow to the squadron.

He was more than a mere member of the squadron; you might almost say that he was the foundation stone upon which it was first formed and built. He was one of the first people to join the squadron when it was started, and he was, I think, easily the outstanding personality of us all. I don't think anybody could mention 609 without immediately thinking of Pip, and his death in the face of such overwhelming odds was characteristic of his brave and resolute spirit.

I admired the C.O. very much in these difficult days. He flew as much as everybody else, never batted an eyelid, and remained as imperturbable and serene as ever.

It was a very fine example of what can be done by one man's courage and determination, and very shortly matters began to improve, as other fighter squadrons were sent to the south-west to reinforce us.

The lesson about going out in such small numbers had also been learnt, and from now onwards we generally flew as a complete squadron, which is a very much more formidable and powerful adversary than three aircraft only.

Two days later, three of us, Stephen, Jarvis, and myself, took off in cloudy weather to intercept a lone enemy aircraft which was on a reconnaissance flight.

We flew for some minutes on a given course and were then told by Operations Room, "Look out for him now on your left." A moment later both Jarvis and I saw him up in the clouds on our left, just as "operations" had forecast. Stephen, who was leading, did not see him, and so after a few seconds, I broke away from formation and went hard after the Dornier, with Jarvis just behind me.

We opened right up to full throttle, and overhauled the Dornier very rapidly. He didn't see us coming till I was about 400 yards away, and then he turned and ran for the nearest cloud with black smoke coming from both engines as an indication that he also was "flat out".

The rear gunner opened fire at me and I could see his tracers flicking past like little red sparks, but he was very inaccurate, and a moment later I opened fire and am certain that I killed him immediately as there was no more return fire and I saw my bursts going right into the fuselage. Jarvis said later he was certain that I had shot him down, as he also saw my fire going right into the Dornier.

However, the cloud loomed up ahead and a second later the Dornier vanished. I turned left hoping to intercept him on the other side of the cloud, but did not see him again. Jarvis had three short bursts at him in gaps in the cloud, but unfortunately lost him also, and so a rather badly damaged Dornier got away safely. Had the cloud been only half a mile farther away, I think we should have got him easily.

A few days later, news came through that Gordon's body had been washed up near Newport on the Isle of Wight. The station ambulance went down and collected the body, and on Thursday, 25th July, exactly a fortnight after his death, I travelled up in the ambulance to Letchworth to his funeral.

His death had been an overwhelming tragedy for his parents, for he was an only son. I think they felt that after his loss there was really very little left to live for. But they were marvellously brave about it and very kind to me and touchingly grateful for the letter I had written to them, giving all the known details of Gordon's death, and the approximate time it occurred, etc.

The service was short and simple, and he was buried in a lovely little country church near Letchworth. Mr. Bisseker, our old headmaster and a very old friend of the Mitchells, came over from Cambridge to conduct the service.

I went up to London after the funeral and spent the night at Hampstead with Dorothy, and returned to the squadron the next day.

★ ★ ★

All through July and early August we used to get regularly the unpopular task of escorting convoys up and down the Channel.

The Germans at that time were concentrating mainly on attacking shipping rather than land objectives, and some very fierce fights used to occur when they bombed the ships.

We all disliked this work; the weather was brilliant and the Huns invariably used to attack out of the sun, and sometimes took the escorting fighters completely by surprise.

Also we were always outnumbered, sometimes by ridiculous odds, and a lot of pilots were lost. Some of these were drowned, without doubt, when their machine was hit and they descended in the water ten or fifteen miles from land, and were not found despite all the searching that took place afterwards.

Two days after Gordon's funeral, on 27th July, a convoy was lying in Weymouth Bay when a German formation approached, and we went out to intercept it. A very confused action followed, in which most of us never saw or engaged the enemy, but we lost one pilot, Buck, who was almost certainly shot down by Me. 109s.

Johnny and I could never quite understand what happened to him, because he was leading us in Green Section and we were turning all round behind him, guarding his tail while we patrolled. We both turned away to have a good look behind, and when we turned again he had vanished quite suddenly, and we never saw him again, though we stayed together for the rest of the patrol. Neither of us saw any Huns near us, though there were a lot of Me. 109s some distance above, and we came to the conclusion that he must have seen a Ju. 87 in the broken clouds just below us and dived down immediately to attack it and then been shot down. But we both felt rather unhappy about it, although there was certainly nothing that we could have done to prevent it, and he was definitely not shot down while he was with us.

Johnny and I went out to search for him afterwards and saw something in the water, so we directed a patrol boat to it as it looked like a parachute, but actually it was a stray barrage balloon. As a matter of fact, no trace of Buck was ever found.

We stayed out there for nearly an hour, circling round very low on the water, till the boat arrived to confirm that it was a barrage balloon, and I was quite thankful to get back again afterwards, as we were forty or fifty miles out to sea, very near the French coast, and at the mercy of any Me. 109s that happened to see us. But fortunately none of them appeared.

I think Buck's death also was very largely due to inexperience and faulty tactics. We had not yet learnt that it did not pay to go out to sea to meet the enemy, but to let them come to us. Also we did not realize the importance that height meant. Afterwards we used to get as high as possible before going into action. This is the whole secret of success in air fighting.

But Buck's death was another in the series of unnecessary losses, against which we had very little to show in the way of success, and I think that we all felt depressed and discouraged. He was a jolly good chap and a sound pilot.

However, we learnt our lesson from these deaths, though it seems so grim that in a war experience is almost always gained at the expense of other men's lives. But the end of July came, and with it the end of our bad luck.

August was to produce many successes and at least one brilliant victory.

AUGUST–SEPTEMBER

On 29th July I got some leave, and so Dorothy and I went up to Huddersfield, where we spent four happy days and managed to see quite a lot of people. On the last day of my leave we returned to London, where we had a good dinner, saw Leslie Henson's show, and altogether enjoyed the evening very much indeed.

There were several changes in the squadron when I got back. We had a new Flight Commander in B Flight, Mac, who had been a test pilot at Farnborough for two years. Before that he had done a lot of civil flying, including some long-distance flights with Campbell Black, and, as a matter of fact, Mac still holds the London- Baghdad record. There were also several other new pilots, including two Poles and three Americans, and altogether the flying personnel of the squadron were now a very young, vigorous, and dashing crowd. I think that this influx of new blood played a big part in bringing to an end our run of bad luck, because from now onwards we started on an almost unbroken series of successes and victories.

But in less than a year 609 had altered completely its personnel and character. We had a new C.O., and of the fifteen original members of the squadron, only four were now left.

Four others had been posted away as instructors and seven had been killed at Dunkirk or later. Only Michael, John, and myself were left, and we were joined a few days later by Geoff who had just finished his course at Cranwell. It was grand to have him back, and so for the next six weeks we flew together and went out on most evenings to the "Mucky Duck" for a little beer, and altogether enjoyed life, in spite of the intense air activity that prevailed.

The first week of August 1940 was very quiet indeed, and apart from a few enemy machines that flew over at a great height for reconnaissance and photography, nothing stirred at all. We used to go up after these machines and chase after them over most of south-western England, but they always flew so high and so fast that we were never able to make any interceptions, or even to see one. It is not till you go hunting after single machines like this that you realize the vastness of the sky, and how easy it is, even on a clear day, to miss one aircraft or even a whole squadron, in the enormous spaces above.

We had a private and somewhat jocular theory that this unnatural peace was due to Goering having given the whole German Air Force a week's leave to get them fit for "things to come".

Certainly it was the lull before the storm.

The Intelligence reports that we got told of the efforts the Germans were making to establish themselves at all the captured aerodromes in northern

France, Holland, and Belgium, and obviously preparations were being made on the very greatest scale in order to launch a very heavy air offensive against this country.

I don't know whether many people yet realize fully the great strategical advantages gained by Germany through her occupation of the Low Countries and France.

Hitherto, the Germans had been forced to fly big distances in order to reach this country, whereas we possessed advanced bases in France from which it was only a short flight into the heart of the enemy industrial areas. But we never used these advantages when they were in our grasp, and for the first eight months of the war, there was no bombing of land targets by either side.

When the big German attack was launched in the west, the tables were turned immediately. We lost our advanced bases, and the enemy gained theirs. Nor was this the end of the misfortunes that fell upon us as a result of the disasters in France. A very big proportion of the German Air Force is composed of Messerschmidt 109s and Junkers 87 dive-bombers, both of which are essentially short-range machines, and could not possibly operate against England from German bases. But their weight could now be thrown into the struggle, and so, instead of meeting Heinkel and Dornier bombers over this country, and being able to inflict wholesale slaughter on them, we had to face very large numbers of escorting Messerschmidts, which had to be tackled first. This made the work of our fighter squadrons very much more difficult and dangerous, and certainly saved the Germans from the murderous losses which they would have suffered had they sent over unescorted bombers.

Anyway, as it turned out, even their escorting fighters did not manage to save the bombers, and large numbers were shot down.

And so we enjoyed our few days of peace, and did quite a lot of practice flying and attacks, and waited for the storm to break.

At this time we were still working under an arrangement whereby we lived at our base and spent every third day down at the advanced base. We took it in turns with two other squadrons.

On 8th August, soon after dawn, we were ordered to patrol a convoy off the Needles. It was a very clear day with a brilliant sun — just the sort of day that the Germans love, because they come out at a very big height and dive down to attack out of the sun. By doing this cleverly, they used to render themselves almost invisible until the attack was delivered. We hated these clear days and always prayed for some high cloud to cover the sun.

This convoy was a big one and escorted by several destroyers and balloons towed from barges in order to stop low dive-bombing.

I remember thinking at the time that there was obviously going to be a lot of trouble that day, because this convoy was far too large a prize for the Hun to miss. How right I was!

However, nothing happened on our first patrol and after about an hour we returned to base.

About 11.30 a.m. six of us were ordered off again, but one turned back almost immediately with oxygen trouble, so there were only five left.

We steered out towards the convoy, which was now about twelve miles south of Bournemouth. There was a small layer of cloud, and while dodging in and out of this, Mac and I got separated from the other three, and a moment later we also lost each other.

While looking around to try and find them, I glanced out towards the convoy, and saw three of the balloons falling in flames. Obviously an attack was starting, and I climbed above the cloud layer and went towards the convoy at full throttle, climbing all the time towards the sun, so that I could deliver my attack with the sun behind me.

I was now about five miles from the convoy, and could see a big number of enemy fighters circling above, looking exactly like a swarm of flies buzzing round a pot of jam. Below them the dive-bombers were diving down on the ships and great fountains of white foam were springing up where their bombs struck the water. I could see that one or two ships had already been hit and were on fire.

I was now at 16,000 feet above the whole battle and turned round to look for a victim. At that moment, a Hurricane squadron appeared on the scene, and attacked right into the middle of the enemy fighters, which were split up immediately, and a whole series of individual combats started covering a very big area of the sky.

I saw several machines diving down with smoke and flames pouring from them, and then I spotted an Me. 109 flying about 4,000 feet below me. I immediately turned and dived down on him — he was a sitting target, but before I got to him a Hurricane appeared and shot him down in flames.

I was annoyed! I looked round, but the attack was finished, and the enemy were streaming back towards the French coast, where it was very unwise to follow them.

Three ships in the convoy were blazing away fiercely and destroyers were taking off the crews. All the balloons had been shot down. I turned back for the English coast and landed at base, to find everybody back safely. The C.O., Michael, and John had each destroyed an Me. 110, while Mac had shot down two Junkers 87 dive-bombers. He would have got an Me. 110 also and got his sights on it, but nothing happened when he pressed his trigger. His ammunition was finished. So a very lucky Me. 110 lived to fight another day.

Mac was very pleased about this fight, and certainly a bag of two for one's first action is very good. But it made him rather over-confident, and for the next few days he regarded the German Air Force rather as an organization which provided him with a little target practice and general harmless amusement. He soon learnt better!

That evening, when we again patrolled the convoy, he led Michael and me almost over Cherbourg in search of enemy fighters and frightened us considerably! Finally I called him up on the R.T., and politely pointed out that we were now fifty miles out to sea and that the French coast was looming up ahead. So he turned back with great reluctance!

On 11th August there occurred our first really big action of the war. We were again down at advanced base, and about 11.30a.m. we were ordered to patrol over Weymouth Bay. Several other squadrons soon joined us, and altogether it looked as though it was going to be a big show.

Shortly afterwards we saw a big enemy fighter formation out to sea, and went out to attack it, climbing the whole time, as they were flying at about 24,000 feet. Some Hurricanes were already attacking the Messerschmidts, and the latter had formed their usual defensive circle, going round and round on each other's tails. This makes an attack rather difficult, as if you attack one Hun, there is always another one behind you. We were now about a thousand feet above the Me.s at 25,000 feet, and the C.O. turned round and the whole of 609 went down to attack.

We came down right on top of the enemy formation, going at terrific speed, and as we approached them we split up slightly, each pilot selecting his own target.

I saw an Me. 110 ahead of me going across in front. I fired at him but did not allow enough deflection and my bullets passed behind him. I then closed in on him from behind and fired a good burst at practically point-blank range. Some black smoke poured from his port engine and he turned up to the right and stalled. I could not see what happened after this as I narrowly missed hitting his port wing. It flashed past so close that instinctively I ducked my head.

There were many more enemy fighters above me and a terrific fight was going on. I couldn't see another target in a good position for me to attack, and it was rather an unhealthy spot in which to linger so I turned and dived back to the coast and landed to refuel and rearm.

Everybody came streaming back in ones and twos, and to my surprise nobody was missing. It seemed too good to be true that we should all be safe after such a fierce scrap. We had shot down about five Me. 110s and several more (like mine) were probably destroyed, but it is almost impossible to stay and see definite results in the middle of such a mix-up. All that you can do is to fire a good burst at some enemy and then, hit or miss, get away quickly.

Some bombers had got through to Weymouth and Portland, and there was a great column of smoke rising from a blazing oil tank, but no very serious damage had been done. The Germans, in spite of their great numerical superiority, had suffered considerable losses.

Mac came back feeling rather shaken. He had not shot anything down, but had been attacked by two Me.s and in his efforts to get away, his Spitfire got into a spin and he came down about 6,000 feet before he could recover.

From now onwards he was a very wise and successful Flight Commander, and never went out looking for unnecessary trouble!

The following day, 12th August, a very heavy attack was made on Portsmouth and the dockyard. At midday I was due for twenty-four hours' leave and I was having a bath and shave in my room at about 11 a.m. when somebody rushed up and said that we had been called to readiness. I hastily wiped the soap off my face and we all jumped into cars and went down to our aircraft.

A moment later the order came through to take off and patrol Portsmouth and the Isle of Wight. Just as we were taxi-ing out, I switched on my R.T. and found it was dead. The rest of the squadron took off, and I sat on the ground for nearly five minutes till the loose connection was found and put right. I then took off and headed for the Isle of Wight, but could see no sign of the squadron, and, as a matter of fact, I did not see them again for the whole of the action.

After a few minutes I saw a big A.A. barrage going up over Portsmouth, so I turned slightly in that direction. The dockyard at Portsmouth had been hit and I could see one or two big fires going.

A powerful force of German aircraft was circling over the east end of the Isle of Wight, and I went out towards them, climbing all the time. As I got nearer, I was staggered by the number of Huns in the sky. I think we had always imagined that raids might be carried out by three or four squadrons at the most — some forty or fifty aircraft.

And here, circling and sweeping all over the sky, were at least 200 Huns! "My God," I muttered to myself, "what a party." I was not the only person to be impressed. Several other people (not only in 609) who were also in this fight told me afterwards that their main impression had been one of blank astonishment at the numbers of aircraft involved. As somebody remarked — "There was the whole German Air Force, bar Goering." Later in the summer we got used to seeing these enormous formations, but this first occasion certainly made us think a bit.

I climbed out towards the Huns and saw three formations of Messerschmidts circling round, one above the other, between about 20,000 and 28,000 feet. Each layer had formed into the usual German defensive circle, going round and round on each other's tails. I decided to attack the middle layer, which was composed of Me. 110s, as I did not like the idea of continuing to climb up more or less directly underneath the top layer.

I got into position about 2,000 feet above the Me. 110s and then dived straight down into the middle of the circle. As I was going down I selected a target and blazed away madly at him, missing him at first owing to lack of deflection, and then, as far as I could see, getting in a few seconds' effective fire at very close range.

But I could not observe any results as I flashed right through the enemy formation at terrific speed, narrowly missing a collision with one fighter and continuing my dive for some distance before I could pull out. I think I was doing well over 500 m.p.h. and the strain of pulling out was considerable.

I looked round to see what was going on, and at that moment an Me. 110, enveloped in a sheet of flame, fell past within 200 yards of me. I don't know if this was my victim or not, but I definitely think it was, as I had seen no other British fighters in the vicinity when I attacked. There were a lot of Huns all round and above me, and I decided it might be a good idea if I moved on elsewhere, particularly as I had very little ammunition left.

So I turned on my back and dived away to the English coast, and shortly afterwards landed safely at the aerodrome.

Once again everybody got back safely, and we had destroyed six or seven Huns and several more probables, including mine.

My dive through the Hun circle had been so fast and the pull out so violent (probably in the heat of the moment I pulled out far more quickly than I realized), that as a result both wings of my Spitfire were damaged and she had to go back to the factory for repairs. So I reckon I must have been going fairly fast.

Most of the squadron got rather split up at the beginning of the fight and adopted the same tactics as I did, i.e. diving through the Hun circles and trying to pick off a target as they went down.

It was a boiling summer's day and we all got back absolutely soaked in sweat, even though we were flying in shirt sleeves.

Teeny, having fired off all his ammunition, landed at a near-by aerodrome to refuel and rearm, and while the airmen were doing this he decided that he had earned a good drink. So he borrowed a bicycle and started off for the mess. While on his way he saw another Spitfire land and the second pilot also leapt on to a bicycle and pedalled hard towards the mess.

This was John, and the two met on the steps of the mess and without saying a word they went straight in and drank a pint of iced Pimms apiece, after which they felt much better and swapped experiences.

That afternoon, about 4 o'clock, Mac, Noel, and I had changed our clothes and made out our combat reports, so we started at last on our journey up to Town, about five hours later than we had intended.

The car wasn't going very well, and near Staines it packed up for about half an hour while we cursed like hell and Mac fiddled with the petrol pump. I was rather worried as I had arranged to meet Dorothy in the Trocadero at 6.30 and knew I should be late and that therefore she would be having a very unpleasant time wondering if anything had happened. I could not ring up, however, as the delay was so great, so I just had to hope for the best. Finally I got a lift from a couple of Canadian officers, and Mac and Noel promised to follow in the car as soon as it would work. So I arrived at the Troc about an hour and a half late and found D. there with Michael, who had left the aerodrome early in the morning, as he had the whole day off.

Poor D. She was very worried about my non-arrival, and Michael could give her no news except that he thought another big fight was starting just as he left. She must have had many bad moments through the summer, but she always says that this was easily the worst. Anyway, we all had several Pimms apiece and felt much better, and shortly afterwards Mac and Noel arrived, having at last coaxed the car into activity.

We had a hilarious dinner together, and parted in very good form about 11.30 pm.

It seemed so funny to be dining peacefully in Piccadilly only a few hours after being in such a desperate fight.

The following morning I met Michael in Piccadilly and we drove back together.

At midday the squadron flew down to advanced base. The date was 13th August — a very lucky thirteenth for us, as it happened.

At about 4p.m. we were ordered to patrol Weymouth at 15,000 feet. We took off, thirteen machines in all, with the C.O. leading, and climbed up over Weymouth. After a few minutes I began to hear a German voice talking on the R.T., faintly at first and then growing in volume. By a curious chance this German raid had a wavelength almost identical with our own and the voice we heard was that of the German Commander talking to his formation as they approached us across the Channel. About a quarter of an hour later we saw a large German formation approaching below us. There were a number of Junkers 87 dive-bombers escorted by Me. 109s above, and also some Me. 110s about two miles behind, some sixty machines in all.

A Hurricane squadron attacked the Me. 110s as soon as they crossed the coast and they never got through to where we were.

Meanwhile the bombers with their fighter escort still circling above them, passed beneath us. We were up at almost 20,000 feet in the sun and I don't think they ever saw us till the very last moment. The C.O. gave a terrific "Tally ho" and led us round in a big semi-circle so that we were now behind them, and we prepared to attack.

Mac, Novi (one of the Poles), and I were flying slightly behind and above the rest of the squadron, guarding their tails, and at this moment I saw about five Me. 109s pass just underneath us.

I immediately broke away from the formation, dived on to the last Me. 109, and gave him a terrific burst of fire at very close range. He burst into flames and spun down for many thousands of feet into the clouds below, leaving behind him a long trail of black smoke.

I followed him down for some way and could not pull out of my dive in time to avoid going below the clouds myself. I found that I was about five miles north of Weymouth, and then I saw a great column of smoke rising from the ground a short distance away. I knew perfectly well what it was and went over to have a look. My Me. 109 lay in a field, a tangled heap of wreckage burning fiercely, but with the black crosses on the wings still visible. I found out later that the pilot was still in the machine. He had made no attempt to get out while the aircraft was diving and he had obviously been killed by my first burst of fire. He crashed just outside a small village, and I could see everybody streaming out of their houses and rushing to the spot.

I climbed up through the clouds again to rejoin the fight, but there was nothing to be seen, and so I returned to the aerodrome, where all the ground crews were in a great state of excitement, as they could hear a terrific fight going on above the clouds but saw nothing except several German machines falling in flames.

All the machines were now coming in to land and everybody's eyes were fixed on the wings.

Yes — they were all covered with black streaks from the smoke of the guns — everybody had fired.

There was the usual anxious counting — only ten back — where are the others — they should be back by now — I hope to God everybody's O.K. — good enough, here they come! Thank God, everybody's O.K.!

We all stood round in small groups talking excitedly, and exchanging experiences. It is very amusing to observe the exhilaration and excitement which everybody betrays after a successful action like this!

It soon became obvious that this had been our best effort yet.

Thirteen enemy machines had been destroyed in about four minutes' glorious fighting. Six more were probably destroyed or damaged, while our only damage sustained was one bullet through somebody's wing. I think this was the record bag for one squadron in one fight during the whole of the Battle of Britain.

Just after I broke away to attack my Messerschmidt, the whole squadron had dived right into the centre of the German formation and the massacre started. One pilot looked round in the middle of the action and in one small patch of sky he saw five German dive-bombers going down in flames, still more or less in formation.

We all heard the German commander saying desperately, time after time, "Achtung, achtung, Spit und Hurri" — meaning presumably, "Look out, look out, Spitfires and Hurricanes."

Novi got two Me. 109s in his first fight and came back more pleased with himself and more excited than I have ever seen anybody before.

And so ended this very successful day, the thirteenth day of the month, and thirteen of our pilots went into action, and thirteen of the enemy were shot down. I shall never again distrust the number 13.

One member of the squadron remarked afterwards that he rather missed the "glorious twelfth" this year — "but the glorious thirteenth was the best day's shooting I ever had".[1]

---

[1] From *The Times*, 14th August 1940: "In the Southampton area alone fighter patrols destroyed twenty-two of the enemy. Of these, nine were Ju. 87 dive-bombers, five were Me. 110s, and the remaining eight were Messerschmidt 109 fighters. All the nine Junkers were brought down in the space of a few minutes by a single Spitfire squadron, as well as four of the Me. 109s. This same squadron had brought down seven enemy aircraft the previous day. Many others attacked were severely damaged. Not one of the squadron's pilots or Spitfires was lost during the two days' fighting."

I think that 13th August marked a very definite turning-point in the squadron's history. Hitherto we had not had many successes, but had suffered rather heavy losses, and this state of affairs always shakes confidence. But now, for the first time, the glorious realization dawned on us that by using clever and careful tactics we could inflict heavy losses on the enemy and get away almost scot-free ourselves. Whenever in the future the squadron went into action, I think the only question in everybody's mind was not "Shall we get any Huns to-day?" but rather, "How many shall we get today?" There was never any doubt about it. This success was also a very well-deserved tonic for all the airmen in the squadron who did not get all the excitement that we did. They were a grand crowd in 609, mostly the original Auxiliaries who were at Yeadon before the war, and they used to toil nobly in order to keep all our Spitfires serviceable. Frequently in those hectic days they would work all through the night in order to have a machine ready for dawn. Their loyalty to the squadron and their keenness and energy knew no bounds, and as a result we always had the very comforting feeling that our Spitfires were maintained as perfectly as was humanly possible. I don't think my engine ever missed a beat throughout the whole summer, and this means a terrific lot to you when you are continually going into action and any mechanical failure will have the most unpleasant consequences.

All the men are extremely interested in the fortunes of the squadron and particularly the pilot of the machine which they look after. When you return after an action they always crowd round asking for details, and if you can tell them "One Messerschmidt down" then there is great rejoicing. Altogether, from this time onwards, 609 was an exceedingly good squadron and probably second to none in the whole R.A.F.

The following day was very cloudy, and soon after lunch the air-raid warning sounded, and we all dashed out of the mess and went down to the point where our Spitfires were.

There were no orders for us to take off, though three of our machines were already in the air and circling round the aerodrome.

So we sat in our aircraft and waited. A few minutes later we heard the unmistakable "ooma-ooma" of a German bomber above the clouds. I immediately signalled to my ground crew to stand by, as I did not intend to sit on the ground and be bombed. I kept my finger on the engine starter button and waited expectantly.

Almost immediately the enemy bomber, a Junkers 88, broke out of the cloud to the north of the aerodrome, turned slightly to get on his course and then dived at very high speed towards the hangars. At about 1,500 feet he let go four bombs — we could see them very distinctly as they plunged down, and a second later there was an earth-shaking "whoom" and four great clouds of dust arose. All this happened in a matter of seconds only, but by this time everybody had got their engines started and we all roared helter-skelter across the aerodrome. Why there were no collisions I don't know, but we got safely into the air and turned round to chase the enemy.

But this was unnecessary. Sergeant F. had already been in the air, and attacked the enemy just as he was climbing up after releasing his bombs. F. fired all his ammunition at close range and the Junkers crashed in flames about five miles away, all the crew being killed. I flew over to the crash and have never seen any aeroplane more thoroughly wrecked; it was an awful mess.

I certainly admire that German pilot for his coolness and determination, because he made his attack despite the Spitfires that were closing in on him. It was a very daring piece of work, even though he only lived about thirty seconds afterwards to enjoy his triumph.

For the rest of the afternoon we had a very exciting and busy time, as various Huns were coming over in the clouds to bomb us. I was able to engage two of them; in each case I spotted them just as they were breaking from cloud and got a good burst at each before they disappeared again.

They were both certainly damaged, but nothing more. The main thing was that it stopped them bombing the aerodrome, but during the afternoon one other German managed to drop his bombs and get back into cloud again before any of us could intercept him.

We destroyed two definitely, but unfortunately when everybody landed later that evening, G. was missing, and he never turned up. We could not understand this, as all the fights had taken place quite near home and they had been so scrappy and disjointed that it seemed almost impossible for anybody (except Huns) to be killed.

However, the mystery was solved about ten days later, when his body was washed ashore on the Isle of Wight. Obviously he had chased some bomber out to sea and been shot down.

It was a great pity; for his younger brother, also in the R.A.F., had been killed only six weeks before.

Incidentally, in one of the Heinkels shot down three very senior officers of the German Air Force were found dead. They had probably come over to see how the operations against England were progressing.

I hope they were suitably impressed!

The following day, 15th August, we had another raid in the late afternoon, this time by a fairly big formation of Junkers 88s and Me. 110s.

We got off the ground only a few minutes before they arrived at the aerodrome, and were unable to intercept them, or even to see them until they were practically over the aerodrome, as they dived out of the sun, dropped their bombs, and then streamed back towards the coast as hard as they could go. But we were attacking them the whole time and shot down at least five. Oddly enough, less damage was done to the aerodrome by this large raid than on the previous day, when only single machines came over.

Most of these German bomber formations rely on one very good bomb-aimer in the leading machine. When he gets his sights on, the whole formation release their bombs and if the aim is accurate, the effect is generally rather devastating, but on this occasion the bomb-aimer misjudged by about two seconds and the whole salvo of bombs fell just beyond the aerodrome.

This occasion was the now famous one when I shot down one of our own machines — a Blenheim.

There was a Blenheim fighter squadron stationed with us; they are not fast enough for day fighting but are used a lot for night work. Incidentally, they are twin-engined machines and very similar in appearance to the Junkers 88.

One of these Blenheims happened to be doing some practice flying near the aerodrome when the attack started, and in a fit of rather misguided valour he fastened himself on to the German formation as it ran for the coast and started attacking the rear machines.

We were rapidly overhauling the German formation, and when I was in range I opened fire at the nearest machine, which happened to be the Blenheim.

Quite naturally, it never occurred to me that it could be anything else but a Ju. 88. I hit both engines and the fuselage, and he fell away to the right with one engine smoking furiously. I saw him gliding down and noticed a gun turret on the fuselage which rather shook me, as I knew the Ju. 88 did not have this.

Fortunately the pilot had been saved by the armour plating behind him, and he managed to make a crash landing on the aerodrome and was quite O.K., though the Blenheim was full of bullet holes and looked rather like a kitchen sieve. The rear-gunner was not quite so lucky, for he got a bullet through his bottom which doubtless caused him considerable discomfort and annoyance, but was not serious.

Nothing was said about this mistake, as it certainly was not my fault, and equally the Blenheim pilot could scarcely be blamed for his desire to engage the enemy, even though it was rather unwise, since his machine was so similar to the Germans.

The Blenheims had sometimes got in our way before, and we had often remarked jokingly, "If one of those blasted Blenheims gets in our way again we'll jolly well put a bullet through his bottom." And now it had come to pass, and everybody was very amused (except possibly the rear-gunner).

The whole story became very well known and I was ragged about it for a long time afterwards.

Our other Polish pilot, Osti, distinguished himself in this action. He chased an Me. 110 which in its efforts to shake him off dived to ground level and dodged all over the countryside at over 500 m.p.h., even turning round a church steeple. But Osti stuck to him and refused to be shaken off, and finally the German, as a last desperate resort, flew right through the Southampton balloon barrage.

Osti went through after him, caught him up over the Solent, and shot him down in the Isle of Wight.

These two Poles, Novi and Osti, were grand chaps and we were all very fond of them. They had fought in Poland during that desperate month of September 1939, when in spite of inferior equipment and being hopelessly outnumbered, they nevertheless resisted to the bitter end, and then escaped through Rumania to

France, where they joined l'Armée de l'Air, and again fought till the French collapse, though they were shabbily treated by the French, who gave them only very obsolete machines to fly.

They told us some astounding stories about conditions in France during the disasters in May and June.

They were stationed near Tours, and on the aerodrome were a number of very good new American Curtis fighters. The Poles, who had been given Moranes which were old and hardly fit to fly, begged to be allowed to fly the Curtis's.

But the French refused, saying they wanted the Curtis's themselves.

Every day the Germans used to fly serenely over Tours, bomb the city at leisure and fly back again, while nobody raised a finger to stop them, and the French pilots sat in the bar and drank their vermouth, with a lot of brand new fighters standing on the aerodrome outside. Incredible but true.

After the French collapse Novi and Osti and several thousand more of their indomitable countrymen escaped once more from a ravaged country and came over to England. It is easy to imagine their pleasure at finding themselves in a really good squadron, efficiently run, and with first-class equipment. They could now fly the finest fighters in the world, and meet their persecutors on equal terms.

They certainly made the most of their opportunities, and their delight when they shot down a "bloddy German" was marvellous to see.

They were both very quiet, possessed beautiful manners, were very good pilots, and intensely keen to learn our ways and methods. Their hatred of the Germans was quieter and more deadly than I have ever seen before.

They had undergone so much suffering and hardship, and had lost almost everything in life that mattered to them — homes, families, money — that I think the only thing that concerned them now was to get their revenge and kill as many Germans as possible.

They were certainly two of the bravest people I ever knew, and yet they were not exceptional in this respect when compared with other Poles in the R.A.F.

All the squadrons that had Polish pilots posted to them formed an equally high opinion of them, and the feats of the Polish Squadron, who in five days' fighting over London destroyed at least forty-four German machines, as well as probably destroying and damaging many more, must rank as one of the best shows of the whole summer.

Such indomitable courage and determination cannot go unrewarded, and when this war is won we must see that Poland is again restored to her former liberty and freedom, which her sons fought so valiantly to maintain.

After this raid life became much quieter for a short period, and while we had a number of alarms and went up on patrol quite a lot, we did not come into contact with the enemy for some little time to come.

In the middle of our "busy time", when every day seemed to bring a bigger and heavier raid to deal with, we used to long for bad weather to come and give us some relief. Now when matters became quieter and we had no fighting, we all got very bored after a few days and longed to shoot down some more Huns. Human nature is never satisfied for long.

I was still managing to get up to London once or twice a week to meet Dorothy. We used to have some enjoyable dinners, sometimes with Michael and Geoff when they were up in town also.

Serious bombing had not yet commenced in London, and life was still proceeding much as usual, so after dinner we used to go to a flick or a show and then back to Hampstead for the night. I always had to leave in fairly good time in the morning in order to catch the train from Waterloo.

On 23rd August I managed to get my twenty-four hours' leave as usual, and met Dorothy to celebrate the first anniversary of our wedding. We had a good dinner at Hatchett's, listened to an excellent band, and altogether enjoyed our little celebration.

What an eventful year it had been! But in spite of all the worries and anxieties of the present, I think we both felt much happier and more confident than we had done a year previously, when we were married under the shadow of impending war and the whole future seemed so black and full of doubt.

It was still equally uncertain now, but we were getting more accustomed to the idea of never thinking about the future (one never dared to hope for a future in those days), and we had made the necessary mental adjustments to be able to face the worries and doubts.

In this year there had been so much personal happiness, and such good times, so many outstanding people met, and so many new friends made.

There had been the finest flying I have ever had, and the most exciting and wildly exhilarating moments of my life, such as the fight over Weymouth and that first engagement with the enemy when I dived on to the Junkers 87 and sent it crashing down in flames into the sea.

And on the other hand, there had been so much monotony and anxiety, both inevitable in war, and in the latter part of the year there occurred the tragic deaths of so many gallant friends, among them being some of the finest people I ever knew.

But on the whole it had been easily the happiest and the most vivid year of my life. I certainly could not feel now (as I used to feel occasionally before the war) that I should lead an uneventful life and grow into an old man without possessing any really exciting and stirring memories to gladden my old age!

The following day, 24th August, I returned to the squadron. The weather was brilliantly clear again, to our intense disgust, and we anticipated a lot more trouble.

Mac was very amusing on the subject of the weather, and always used to scan the sky anxiously, looking for clouds. When we saw any rolling up, he would express great satisfaction and announce that it might keep the

"Grim Reaper" at bay for another few days. Mac and his "Grim Reaper" became a stock joke, and if anybody had a very narrow escape, we always used to congratulate them on keeping the "Grim Reaper" at bay.

Certainly it was typical of our English weather that in a normal summer it is quite impossible to get fine weather for one's holidays, and yet in war time, when every fine day simply plays into the hands of the German bombers, we had week after week of cloudless blue skies.

24th August proved to be no exception to the general rule, and about 4p.m. we took off with orders to patrol Portsmouth at 10,000 feet. A number of other squadrons were also operating, each at different heights, and on this occasion we were the luckless ones sent low down to deal with any possible dive-bombers.

We hated this — it's a much more comforting and reassuring feeling to be on top of everything than right underneath. Superior height, as I said before, is the whole secret of success in air fighting.

However, "orders is orders" and so we patrolled Portsmouth. Very soon a terrific A.A. barrage sprang up ahead of us, looking exactly like a large number of dirty cotton-wool puffs in the sky. It was a most impressive barrage; besides all the guns at Portsmouth, all the warships in the harbour and dockyard were firing hard.

A moment later, through the barrage and well above us, we saw a large German formation wheeling above Portsmouth. We were too low to be able to do anything about it, but they were being engaged by the higher squadrons.

They were now releasing their bombs, and I cannot imagine a more flagrant case of indiscriminate bombing. The whole salvo fell right into the middle of Portsmouth, and I could see great spurts of flame and smoke springing up all over the place.

We spent a very unpleasant few minutes right underneath the German formation, praying hard that their fighters would not come down on us.

However, the danger passed and a very disgruntled squadron returned home, having seen so many Huns and yet not having fired a single round.

Also, one of our Americans, Andy, was attacked by an Me. 110 which, in his inexperience, he never saw following him, and the Hun put a lot of bullets into Andy's machine. Fortunately Andy was not hit and managed to bring a battered Spitfire safely home. He was very lucky to get away with it.

These three Americans — "Andy", "Shorty", and "Red", had come over to join the French Air Force. They reached France in May just at the beginning of the German attack, and when things started to crack up they hitch-hiked down to Saint-Jean-de-Luz and got away in the last ship, without being able to get accepted by the French. In London they got a pretty cool reception at the American Embassy, who obviously weren't going to assist them to break the neutrality laws. They even tried to send them back to the States.

But fortunately Red had got an introduction to some M.P. and went along to the House to see him. After that everything went smoothly; twenty-four hours later they were in the R.A.F., and after a short training they came to us. They had been civil pilots in America and had done a lot of flying. But civil flying is one thing and military flying, particularly in war, is quite another, and they were very raw and inexperienced when they came to us. However, they were keen, and soon improved.

They were typical Americans, amusing, always ready with some devastating wisecrack (frequently at the expense of authority), and altogether excellent company. Our three Yanks became quite an outstanding feature of the squadron.

Andy was dark, tough, and certainly rather good-looking with his black hair and flashing eyes.

Red was very tall and lanky, and possessed the most casual manner and general outlook on life that I ever saw. I don't believe he ever batted an eyelid about anything, except possibly the increasing difficulty of getting his favourite "rye high". After a fight he never showed the slightest trace of excitement, and I remember that after one afternoon's fairly concentrated bombing of the aerodrome, during which a number of people were killed, he turned up grinning as usual but with his clothes in an awful mess and covered in white chalk because he had to throw himself several times into a chalk pit as the Huns dropped out of the clouds. He made only the grinning comment, "Aw hell, I had a million laffs!"

Shorty was the smallest man I ever saw, barring circus freaks, but he possessed a very stout size in hearts. When he arrived in the squadron we couldn't

72

believe that he would ever reach the rudder bar in a Spit; apparently the Medical Board thought the same and refused to have him at first, as he was much shorter than the R.A.F. minimum requirements. However, Shorty insisted on having a trial, and he produced two cushions which he had brought all the way from the States via France, specially for this purpose. One went under his parachute and raised him up, the other he wedged in the small of his back, and thus he managed to fly a Spitfire satisfactorily, though in the machine all you could see of him was the top of his head and a couple of eyes peering over the edge of the cockpit.

One day the Duke of Kent came down to see us. The Americans were very intrigued about the forthcoming visit; being good Republicans they are always much impressed by royalty. Shorty said, "Say, what do we call this guy — dook?" We hastily assured him that "sir" would be sufficient. Anyway, the "dook" arrived, shook hands with each of us, and spoke to us, and had a particularly long chat with Shorty, who amongst other jobs in a very varied career, had been a professional parachute jumper. Shorty was immensely gratified.

Unfortunately, after about six weeks with us, and just as they were becoming really good, they were posted away to form the Eagle Squadron. We were very sorry to lose them, because they were grand fellows.

They are all dead now. Shorty was last seen spinning into the sea near Flamborough Head during a chase after a Heinkel. Red crashed behind

Boulogne, fighting like hell against a crowd of Me. 109s, while Andy hit a hill in bad weather and was killed. As Red once remarked with the usual grin, pointing to the wings on his tunic, "I reckon these are a one way ticket, pal."

I think it was a very fine gesture on their part to come over here and help us to fight our battles, and they came at a time when trained pilots were worth a great deal in Fighter Command. They are in the first half-dozen of that small but honourable band of Americans who have already been killed in this war, while serving in the R.A.F.

About this time we received a visit from Lord Trenchard. He seemed remarkably young for a man who commanded the R.A.F. in the last war, and he chatted to us for a long time in a very paternal and charming manner, congratulated us on our successes, and said that the only way to win this war was to give the Hun such hell as he had never had before and would never want again. We all felt that this was remarkably good advice, to be followed whenever possible.

On 25th August we took off in the afternoon and patrolled Swanage as a large German raid was approaching the coast.

Shortly afterwards we sighted a very big German formation coming over the coast below us, and the C.O. swung us into line astern and manoeuvred into a good position for the attack. Then, down we went. I happened to be almost last on the line, and I shall never forget seeing the long line of Spitfires ahead, sweeping down and curling round at terrific speed to strike right into the middle of the German formation. It was superb!

The great weight and fierceness of this onslaught split up the Huns immediately and they scattered all over the place, with Spitfires chasing them right and left. I saw an Me. 110 below me and dived down on him going very fast indeed. Unfortunately I was going too fast and in the heat of the moment I forgot to throttle back, with the result that I came up behind him at terrific speed and overshot him badly. I had a good burst of fire at practically point blank range as he flashed by and then I had to turn away very violently or I should have collided with him.

His rear-gunner took advantage of my mistake and fired a short burst at me, and put several bullets through my wing, very close to the fuselage and only a few inches from my leg.

When I turned round to look for the Hun he had disappeared. Though there was a lot of fighting in progress and machines were turning and diving all over the sky, I had dived down below them all and couldn't do much about it.

A moment later most of the Germans turned out to sea again and chased home.

I went as hard as I could for Weymouth, thinking that I might pick up something there. I got to Weymouth, but the fighting was almost finished there too, although some battle must still have been going on up at a very big height, because one Me. 109 dived vertically down into the sea just off the Chesil Bank and another one with its engine stopped and a Spitfire watching it carefully, glided down and made a forced landing in a field near the coast. I saw the pilot get out quite unhurt, set fire to his machine, and then walk away calmly across the field.

I returned to base absolutely furious with myself for having missed that Me. 110. He was right in front of me, and if only I had not gone at him so wildly I should have had him easily.

Anyway, it taught me to be a little more cool in the future. One lives and one learns — if lucky.

I found that everybody had got back safely and we had destroyed six or seven Huns. Various other squadrons had got some victims also and in all thirty Huns were definitely destroyed on this raid. Bombs had been dropped only at Warmwell, where nobody was hurt, slight damage only was caused, and a few craters made in the aerodrome, which were immediately filled in.

Not a very good return for the loss of thirty machines and crews.

This was Geoff's first action, and he shot down an Me. 110 together with Noel. Officially they were credited with one-half each.

Osti had an amazing escape in this fight. An Me. 110 got on to his tail and put one cannon shell into his engine, where it blew out most of the induction system, while another shell hit the armour plating behind his head, and the explosion almost stunned him.

He managed to get back home with a big hole in his wing as well, but had to land very fast as his flaps were damaged and he ran through the hedge. His machine was a complete "write off", but he was quite O.K., apart from a headache.

Nothing else of interest occurred in the last few days of August, and at the end of the month we were able to add up our score.

This was forty-seven enemy aircraft definitely destroyed, as well as a number of others probably destroyed or damaged, and our only loss was one pilot killed.

This result is astonishing when compared with that of the previous month, July, when in a very few engagements only we lost four pilots and shot down about five Huns — almost equal numbers.

We had now learnt our lessons, though the price of this experience had been the death of several members of the squadron.

We realized now the vital importance of getting above the enemy before going into action; we knew that cool thinking and the element of surprise can more than compensate for inferior numbers, and can sometimes produce astonishing results; we knew from experience that if you attack out of the sun the enemy will hardly ever see you till the last moment; and vice versa, how essential it is to maintain the most intense vigilance always in order to prevent being surprised oneself.

We also realized the importance of constantly dodging and twisting during a fight, because if you steer a straight and steady course for more than about five seconds a Messerschmidt will probably be sitting just behind you and firing as hard as he can.

But after all this, a very great deal of the credit for our changed fortunes was due to the C.O. He came to command the squadron at the beginning of July when, owing to lack of experience, we were not a particularly efficient fighting unit. He was with us all through the bad times when we lost more than we shot down, and when the morale of the squadron might have suffered. But he flew as much as anybody else, led us skilfully, and throughout remained so imperturbable, so confident, and so cheerful that he held us all together by his example.

And so the end of August found us with a very satisfactory and solid background of success and victory, and we now faced the future with an ample confidence that whatever the Germans might do, we could do it far better.

September opened quietly as far as we were concerned, and though we did a number of patrols, nothing much happened. The days were now getting noticeably shorter and we benefited accordingly, as we could now be released at dusk, between 7 p.m. and 8 p.m., and get out more in the evenings.

This was a great contrast with the state of affairs in July, when for several days on end we were on duty (and doing a lot of flying) from 3.30 a.m. till 10.45 p.m.

We were able to do quite a lot of practice flying and I had a lot of dog fights with Geoff. There was a tremendous rivalry between us, and altogether they proved to be most energetic affairs — turning, diving, and climbing all over the sky at anything between 300 m.p.h. and 400 m.p.h. in a desperate attempt to get on each other's tails. But dog fighting in a Spitfire is a very tiring business owing to the high speeds and heavy strains involved, and after about ten minutes we had generally had enough.

So we flew home with honours generally about even, and the loser stood a pint of beer.

At the beginning of the month, the London night bombing started to get rapidly worse, and so rather reluctantly we decided that Dorothy would have to go north to Huddersfield. This was the only thing to do, but it meant the end of our pleasant evenings every week in town. From now onwards we could see each other only on the comparatively rare occasions that I could get up home.

However, on 7th September John and I got the Magister and flew up to Yeadon for twenty-four hours' leave. It seemed very odd to be piloting a little aeroplane at 100 m.p.h. again. I found it more difficult to fly than a Spitfire, so accustomed had I become to the latter.

We did a very neat bit of navigation between us (fighter pilots are not generally renowned for their navigational skill) and dived over John's house at Cawthorne, and flew over Glenwood, where I could see the family waving hard from the lawn.

79

We found everybody in very cheery form when we got back. The first big daylight raid on London had taken place the previous day and 609 had their first fight for about a fortnight, during which time we had become very bored with inactivity. We got about six Huns confirmed, and everybody got back safely (except Noel who had a bullet in his engine and forced-landed). The whole squadron then adjourned to Gordon Harker's cocktail party in aid of the Spitfire Fund.

They all thought this most appropriate! So altogether we had missed quite a lot of fun!

In the next week or two we flew up to London almost every day, sometimes twice a day, in order to give the overworked London squadrons a helping hand. They certainly needed it; the weight and intensity of these raids exceeded anything ever seen before.

Day after day great masses of German bombers with enormous fighter escorts tried to battle their way through to the capital.

Sometimes they were beaten back, sometimes a number of the bombers got through, always they suffered terrible losses.

Day after day, battles of incredible ferocity were taking place, often at a height of five or six miles, and the great conflict raged and thundered through the summer skies of southern England.

Many hundreds of German bombers and fighters littered the fields and countryside, and yet each morning brought a fresh wave of enemy aircraft, manned by crews who generally showed a fine determination and doggedness in the face of such murderous losses.

The strain on everybody in Fighter Command was very heavy indeed during this period. There were so many attacks to meet and so few pilots to do it only a few hundred of us in all, and on many occasions only about half that number were actually engaged. A number of these pilots had only just arrived in squadrons to replace the losses of the previous months. At the end of Dunkirk in June one-quarter of the pilots in Fighter Command had been killed, and now, half-way through September, there were not many left of those who had started the summer's fighting. I think the death of one experienced pilot was a bigger loss to a squadron in those days than ten Spitfires or Hurricanes, because however many fighters we lost or damaged, replacements always turned up immediately. This must have demanded the most terrific efforts from both the factories and the ground crews, and though we couldn't see the efforts we did appreciate the results. But experienced pilots could never be replaced. You could only train the new ones as best you could, keep them out of trouble as much as possible in the air, and hope they would live long enough to gain some experience. Sometimes they did.

The Germans were now making some very heavy attacks on our fighter stations, and many aerodromes were bombed till hardly a building of any importance was left standing, yet they continued to function at full operational efficiency. One or two squadrons lost almost all their pilots in a matter of a few days and had to be withdrawn in order to be rested and reformed. To many pilots in the London squadrons, the strain at times must have seemed almost unbearable, and yet everybody held out, badly outnumbered though they were, and at the end of a few weeks it was the Luftwaffe and not the R.A.F. who had to cry halt.

"Hard pounding, gentlemen," said the Duke of Wellington at Waterloo, "let us see who pounds the longest."

In this prolonged and bitter encounter, it was certainly the R.A.F. who pounded the longest — and the hardest.

We did not get our full share of these battles, however, and though we always went towards London and generally patrolled Guildford or Brooklands, we were often sent off with orders to patrol at a low altitude, about 10,000 feet, in order to deal with any dive-bombing or low-level attacks.

This was quite sensible, as we had a long way to go and might not have had sufficient time to get up to very big altitudes before the Germans arrived. The London squadrons on the other hand, had ample time in which to get up to 26,000 feet or more, and therefore got a lot more fighting than we did, as the enemy bombers used to take full advantage of the cloudless skies and do their bombing from about 18,000 feet, while their escorting fighters circled above them at anything up to 30,000 feet.

It was always a rather tricky and unpleasant business attacking the bombers while their fighter escort were still in position above. Often it was almost impossible to see them because of the blinding sun, but you always knew that they were there, and as soon as they saw a favourable opportunity, they would dive down and attack. Generally, therefore, we had to try to get in one very quick attack on the bombers and then turn round before the fighters arrived on the scene.

Some squadrons used to do head-on attacks at the bombers, approaching them from the opposite direction, firing at them hard in the split seconds as they drew nearer (their aggregate rate of closing being about 550 m.p.h.), and then pull up quickly at the last moment in order to avoid collision. These tactics, carried out with the utmost recklessness and abandon, were generally very successful in destroying some bombers and, more important still, splitting up the formation so that the machines separated, and were then shot down far more easily. Moreover, they rather shook the morale of a number of enemy pilots, and many prisoners, when questioned after capture, said how terrifying they found these attacks.

Certainly, after the offensive had been in progress for a few weeks, enemy bombers showed a much greater tendency to jettison their bombs and turn back when attacked, and this was a great contrast to their earlier showing, when attacks were usually pressed home with the utmost determination.

We were patrolling over south-western London one afternoon in early September, during a big raid, and were watching the sky intently, waiting for the Hun to appear. Suddenly somebody said, "Enemy formation above us on the right."

I looked up and a moment later saw the biggest German bomber formation that I have ever seen. Like a great wedge in the sky, it moved steadily on, black, menacing, apparently irresistible. Above it, a terrific fight was going on between the German fighters and our own squadrons, but nobody apparently had been able to get near the bombers yet. The whole formation had already passed over London from the east, dropped its bombs, and was now running for the coast as hard as it could, being harassed and worried the whole way by our Hurricanes and Spitfires.

We were too low to attack it and started to climb, and a terrific chase took place all the way down to Brighton. But we had too much leeway to be made up over such a short distance, and they crossed the coast before we managed to get into range, though a number were shot down by other squadrons.

I saw one Hurricane pilot, whose machine had been hit, jump out and open his parachute. Immediately four other Hurricanes made straight for him and circled round and round till he reached the ground, watching carefully to see that no enemy fighter shot him in mid-air.

On 13th September I got four days' leave, and accordingly packed my things and prepared to get away at midday. Geoff and Michael had just come back from twenty-four hours in London and I had a chat with them both before leaving. Geoff and I made the usual arrangement that we always made when either of us got leave, that the one who went away would ring the other one's people when he got home and tell them that everything was O.K.

F. and I got into the Magister and started it up, and Geoff having bade me give his love to Dorothy, waved good-bye and wandered down to his Spitfire with Michael to check it over.

My last glimpse of him was very typical: in high spirits after an amusing day with Michael, full of zest and appreciation of life, and looking as fit and pink and massive as he always did.

Together we had had a grand few weeks of flying and fighting, sleeping in deck-chairs in the sun, playing our rough game of cricket, and spending the usual amusing evenings at the Square Club. Geoff had entered into all this with his usual infectious enthusiasm, and I have never seen him so happy or in such excellent form. Certainly, he never had any premonition of death, and up to the very last moments of his life I believe he was as happy, as carefree, and as gay as he always had been.

And thus, with a few casual remarks and jokes, I said goodbye to the person who had been one of my closest friends for the whole of my life.

F. and I took off in the Magister and flew to Peterborough, where I made a somewhat exciting landing in a very high wind and nearly tipped the poor little Magister up on its nose.

F. then continued on his way to London, and I walked to the station, caught a train north, and arrived home a few hours later.

Sunday morning, 15th September, dawned very bright and clear, and I remember thinking when I got up that if the weather in the south was as good as this, then the squadron would probably have a fairly busy day. My guess seemed to have been justified when we heard on the 9p.m. news that there had been a terrific blitz on London, and 185 Huns had been shot down. I wondered how many the squadron had bagged.

The following morning I came into the house just before lunch, and Mother told me that Mrs. Gaunt had just rung up to say that Geoff was reported missing. I immediately wired to Michael asking for information, and he replied saying that Geoff had not come back after a fight over London.

I think that the Gaunts and our family also were still pinning a few last hopes on the word "missing", but I knew perfectly well from previous experience that this merely meant that the body and aircraft had not yet been found or at any rate identified.

I left home the following day and went up to London on my way back to the squadron. I had not been in London since the real "Blitz" started, and found everything changed very much.

By 8p.m. very few people were to be seen in the West End, and the bars and restaurants were doing about one-tenth of their normal trade. However, I met a very amusing Canadian and we had a few beers together.

I said good-bye to my Canadian friend at about 11p.m., and walked back to the hotel through practically deserted streets. I could hear one or two German machines quite plainly and the guns were firing at them rather spasmodically, but the whole business was not nearly as spectacular or as noisy as I had been led to believe. I went to bed and slept soundly all night, despite the fact that John Lewis's and various other stores in Oxford Street were hit that night.

Next morning, after a good night's sleep, bath and shave, I bounced down to breakfast in grand form to find everybody coming up from the shelters looking blear-eyed and dishevelled after a sleepless night. I felt rather guilty!

And so back to the squadron to hear all the known details of Geoff's death.

On 15th September, the day of his death, there had occurred the biggest enemy raids yet experienced, and in terrific battles over London and the south-east, 185 raiders had been definitely destroyed, besides many more probables and damaged. The R.A.F. losses were about twenty-eight fighters, but only twelve pilots, and Geoff had been one of these.

The squadron took off about 11.30 a.m. and flew up to west London. They were then ordered south-east, and at 12.15 they met a very big bomber formation at nearly 20,000 feet over Kenley (just south of Croydon). 609 attacked immediately.

Geoff was one of a section of four machines led by Michael, with Geoff No.2 and two others behind him.

Michael led the section in against the bombers, but could give only a short burst of fire because a lot of Messerschmidts were coming up from the rear to protect the bombers. So Michael broke away very quickly and the last two pilots in the section, Johnny and Shorty (the American) did not even have time to fire but dived away immediately.

They last saw Geoff following Michael into the attack, and after that he was never seen alive again. He had either been hit by one of the rear-gunners in the bombers (Michael came under very heavy fire from them), or more probably, in his intense desire to destroy a bomber, he stayed too long firing at them and was destroyed by the Me. 110s from behind.

Apart from this accident, 609 had quite a good day and destroyed several enemy aircraft. "Ogle", a Canadian, chased a Dornier across London and shot it down near Victoria Station. Incidentally, the Queen of Holland saw this action from her bedroom window and sent a letter of congratulations through her A.D.C. to "Ogle".

The squadron were in action again in the afternoon and over the Channel they caught two Dorniers that had dropped behind the rest of the enemy formation. Michael was leading Green Section and he decided to do a really pansy attack in the approved style, so he gave the order "Green Section, Number One Attack, Number One Attack, Go." He then discovered that there was nobody behind him — they had all dived away and attacked without waiting for orders. So instead of leading a superb charge, he arrived last of all!

The two wretched Dorniers were overwhelmed by the twelve Spitfires and were literally shot to pieces in mid-air. Everybody in B Flight was absolutely determined to have a squirt at the Hun, and as a result there was a mad scramble in which people cut across in front of each other and fired wildly in the direction of the Dorniers, regardless of the fact that the air was full of Spitfires. Fortunately, nobody collected any of the bullets that were flying about, and their energy was duly rewarded as each pilot was able to claim one-sixth of one Dornier very definitely destroyed!

For four days after Geoff's death we heard absolutely no details of the crash or anything. However, on the Thursday, the R.A.F. at Kenley wired to say that the body and Spitfire had been found near there. The crash had been seen by a number of people, but the machine, having fallen for about 20,000 feet, was absolutely smashed and impossible to identify by any number or letter. Geoff's body was identified only by the name in his collar band. He had made no attempt to escape from the machine, though in such a long dive he would have had ample time, had he been alive.

The funeral took place at Huddersfield on 26th September, and I flew up home in order to be present and also to represent the squadron. Unfortunately, however, the Magister had something wrong with one wheel and though one or two men worked nobly to get it right in time, I was rather late in starting. I landed at Yeadon and raced over to Huddersfield by car, and arrived at the church about fifteen minutes after the service had finished. Everybody had gone.

The grave was still open and I walked over to it and stood there for a moment, looking at the inscription on the coffin of this very gallant and delightful friend.

We had known each other all our lives and been at school together for about twelve years, and after that we were in the same squadron. He possessed a most attractive and vital personality, and entered into everything with the utmost keenness and zest; I don't think I have ever known anybody who appeared generally to derive as much enjoyment from life. And what grand times we have had together — the amusing evenings we used to enjoy before the war, those glorious summer days we spent rock-climbing on Scafell and Doe Crag, or sailing unskilfully but with endless amusement in the dinghy on Windermere.

And then, during this last summer, the good days we spent fighting together, having our practice dog fights, playing tip and run, and going out every evening with the rest of the squadron. The memories which I shall always have of Geoff will be those of happiness and laughter and gaiety.

Only a week or two before his death I said to him one evening that if anything were to happen to him, I should feel rather responsible because he was an only son, and I had persuaded him to join the R.A.F. with me. He replied that he would always be grateful to me for my persuasion, because the year that he had spent in the R.A.F. since the beginning of the war had been the best year of his life and he wouldn't have gone into the Army for anything and missed all this glorious fun.

Looking back, I don't think that his death was altogether a surprise to me, because for some time past I had the feeling that he would not survive this war. I had the same feeling about some other friends, notably Basil and Gordon, and two months before Gordon's death I told Dorothy that I was sure he would be killed. She reminded me of this remark soon after she heard of his death.

On the other hand, I am firmly convinced that some other people, Michael for instance, will not be killed. I cannot explain this feeling; it is not based on their qualities as pilots, because they were all good pilots and Geoff particularly so, even though he hadn't much experience of air fighting. But none of us had to start with.

The other fact that impressed me about Geoff's death (and one or two other deaths that occurred soon after) was that they seemed to have no effect on the squadron's spirit. This was a great contrast to the feeling after the casualties at Dunkirk and Weymouth a month or two before. Everybody was naturally very shocked, because Geoff had been so popular, but we were now so consistently successful and strong in our confidence that we had the enemy "just where we wanted him" that nobody was shaken in the least.

But for me it was the biggest loss that I had ever experienced. I could not believe that such a vital spark was now extinguished for ever, and that I would not see him again. I still can't believe it now, sometimes.

I left the churchyard and went down to see the Gaunts.

They were being very brave about it all, but it was an absolutely overwhelming blow to them because he was their only son. It reminded me only too well of Gordon's death — another only son.

Geoff, Gordon, and I were always very pleased to reflect that three Old Leysians should be together in the same squadron. But I was the only one left now.

I had a pleasant journey down next day and flew through Gloucestershire and over the village where our old F.T.S. was. It was all looking as peaceful and sleepy as ever, and I could see the New Inn where we had spent the whole winter, and the village street and Hartwell's garage, and the stream flowing gently through it all. I could even see the orange curtains in our bedroom.

How much had happened since we were all there together! It was only just over four months since we left, and yet it seemed like an age, because so much had happened in that time.

I got back to the squadron to find that I had missed a lot of excitement the previous day. A very big daylight raid had penetrated to Bristol and 609 had been heavily engaged and got quite a good score, about six confirmed with no losses.

A running fight had been taking place from Weymouth, where they crossed the coast, all up through Somerset to Bristol and then back again. A number of our squadrons were engaged and the Germans suffered fairly heavy losses, though I think on the whole they could claim it as a moderately satisfactory raid.

Shortly after my return, a raid approached Southampton and we took off to intercept it. As we were climbing over the Isle of Wight at about 25,000 feet we sighted the German bombers some distance away to the south, a great mass of machines coming steadily on in very good formation. Above them, ranging up to about 35,000 feet, the Me. 109s were circling round and round so that every now and then I could see a quick flash as their wings caught the sun. They were watching us like cats, just waiting for us to attack the bombers, and then the fun would start and it would be the usual hair-raising competition to see if we could get to the bombers before the 109s got to us.

The C.O. swung B Flight into echelon starboard and prepared to do a beam attack. God, I thought, now for it. In that instant somebody shouted "Look out, 109s", and I whipped round just as a whole pack of Messerschmidts tore over our heads not more than thirty feet above us. They came down at terrific speed out of the sun and we never saw them at all till they were on us. We split up in all directions, diving and turning to avoid them. I went down about 2,000 feet, and then looked round and saw a few Spitfires forming up again and chasing some Dorniers out over the Isle of Wight. I went after them as hard as I could, but was about half a mile behind, and as we were all going flat out I didn't seem to get much nearer.

One Dornier was rather behind the rest of the Hun formation, and two black streaks of smoke from his engines showed that he realized his danger and was doing everything he could to catch up. A moment later the leading Spitfire (I learned later that it was Sergeant F.) opened fire on the Dornier and gave him a long burst. The bomber flew steadily on for a moment and then he turned slowly over on his back and started to spin down. We all watched him; it was rather a shaking sight. Down he went, spinning faster and faster at an incredible rate for such a big machine, and then suddenly a wing was wrenched off. The Dornier gave a lurch and continued to dive, but now turning crazily over and over. The crew must have been all dead inside the cabin, for nobody got out. I saw the other wing and the tail break away, and the fuselage then went straight down like a stone and disappeared from sight. A moment later, looking down, I saw a patch of foam appear on the sea over 20,000 feet below, showing where he had dropped.

We turned back for the English coast, as the other Huns were too far away to catch. It had not been a very satisfactory action for us; as a result of the attack by the Me. 109s we were so split up that several people like myself never found a target. However, we got five confirmed destroyed, and very fortunately suffered no casualties. Why those Me. 109s didn't kill half of us in that attack God only knows. They can't have been very good; had the position been reversed and we had dived on them like that, not many of them would have seen the Fatherland again.

Unfortunately, the following day Mac had to go to hospital with ear trouble, and the doctors told him that he would not have to go above 5,000 feet in future. This meant, of course, that he could not remain in a fighter squadron, and poor Mac was very sad about it.

So were we all — he had been a grand chap and an excellent Flight Commander, besides being very successful individually. I am glad to say that he got the D.F.C. a few days later, which bucked him up a lot.

He was the third case of ear trouble that we had in two months. High altitude flying and fighting imposes a very great strain on the ears owing to the rapid changes of pressure when diving from big heights. One day in a fight at nearly 26,000 feet he failed to turn on sufficient oxygen and he lost consciousness almost immediately and woke up again to find he was doing a screaming dive at well over 400 m.p.h. and very near to the ground. He managed to pull out just in time, but he had dived nearly five miles in a few seconds and it was this incident which ruined his ears.

On Friday, 27th September, another big raid tried to get through to Bristol and we took off to intercept. When we sighted the bombers we were too far behind to be able to catch them, but they were very well taken care of by other squadrons.

Also the C.O. had a bad cold and the height caused him such agony in his ears that he had to drop out. He was off flying for over a week as a result of this effort.

Anyway, we continued our patrol, and soon after we saw a squadron of Me. 110s circling over Swanage at 26,000 feet, waiting to protect their bombers on their return. We immediately turned towards the enemy fighters and started to climb above them.

They had formed one of their defensive circles, going round and round on each other's tails — altogether quite a tough nut to crack.

Incidentally this was the first time in this war that we had met the enemy on even terms. Generally we were outnumbered by anything from three to one up to ten to one. But on this glorious occasion there were fifteen of them and twelve of us, and we made the most of it.

We were very close to them now and we started to dive. I think that these moments just before the clash are the most gloriously exciting moments of life. You sit there behind a great engine that seems as vibrant and alive as you are yourself, your thumb waits expectantly on the trigger, and your eyes watch the gun sights through which in a few seconds an enemy will be flying in a veritable hail of fire.

And all round you, in front and behind, there are your friends too, all eager and excited, all thundering down together into the attack! The memory of such moments is burnt into my mind for ever.

I was flying just behind Mick and he turned slightly left to attack an Me. 110 which was coming towards him. But the German was as determined as Mick, and refused to give way or alter course to avoid this head-on attack. Their aggregate speed of closing was at least 600 m.p.h. and an instant later they collided.

There was a terrific explosion and a sheet of flame and black smoke seemed to hang in the air like a great ball of fire. Many little shattered fragments fluttered down, and that was all.

Mick was killed instantly and so were his two German opponents, and hardly any trace of them was ever found.

Poor old Mick! I had known him for a year, as he was at F.T.S. with me. His brother, also in the R.A.F., was killed only two months before in a raid on Germany.

All this happened in an instant, and I turned right in order to get on to the tail of a Hun. My Spitfire immediately went into a very vicious right-hand spin — the atmosphere at these great altitudes is so rarefied that machines are very much more difficult to manoeuvre — and when I recovered I had lost my German.

The whole enemy circle had been broken up by our attack, and various Messerschmidts were streaming out to sea with our people chasing after them.

I saw an Me. 110 about half a mile ahead and went after him on full throttle. He also was going flat out and diving to get extra speed, but my beloved Spitfire rose nobly to the occasion and worked up to over 400 m.p.h., and I caught him fairly easily, though we were about twenty miles out to sea by this time.

The enemy rear-gunner, who obviously had wind up, opened fire at me at rather long range, though I could see his tracer bullets flicking past me. It is an odd thing when you are being fired at by a rear-gunner that the stream of bullets seems to leave the machine very slowly and in a great outward curve. You chuckle to yourself, "Ha, the fool's missing me by miles!" Then, suddenly, the bullets accelerate madly and curl in towards you again and flick just past your head. You thereupon bend your head a little lower, mutter "My God", or some other suitable expression and try to kill the rear-gunner before he makes any more nuisance of himself.

I dived slightly to get underneath his tail, as he could not fire at me in that position, and when in range I opened fire. I must have killed the gunner, because he never fired again, though I must have been visible to him at times and at very close range. I put all my ammunition into the fuselage and port engine and the latter started to smoke furiously. To my intense disgust my ammunition ran out before he went down and I thought that I might have to let him go after all, badly damaged though he was.

I should have been able to shoot him down easily, but on thinking it over afterwards I decided that I must have opened fire too soon — always a temptation during a hard chase — and thus I wasted the first part of my ammunition at too great a range.

But at this moment a voice said on the R.T. "O.K., O.K., help coming," and Bishop gradually overtook us and finished off the Messerschmidt, which fell into the sea. Bishop and I were credited with one-half each in this affair.

Apart from Mick's death, the whole fight had been a great success and six Huns were destroyed and one or two more probables. I bet that German squadron don't look forward to their next trip over England. I know what we should feel like if we were attacked by an equal number of Messerschmidts and half our squadron was destroyed in four minutes.[1]

It's a very good thing to instil into the Hun a healthy respect for the R.A.F.!

I remember walking into the mess for lunch and sitting down and suddenly recollecting that at breakfast, only a few hours before, I had sat next to Mick at this very table and we had chatted together. And now, here we were at the next meal, everything quite normal, and he was dead.

That was the one thing I could never get accustomed to; seeing one's friends gay and full of life as they always were, and then, a few hours later, seeing the batman start packing their kit, their shaving brush still damp from being used that morning, while the owner was lying dead in a shattered aeroplane "somewhere in England".

---

[1] From *The Times*, 28th September 1940: "At one time bombers with escorting fighters crossed the Dorset coast in two waves each of at least fifty machines. They were hotly attacked by A.A. fire and R.A.F. fighters and six were seen to fall in flames. One had a direct hit from an A.A. shell and exploded in the air. Three crashed west of Poole and another fell into the sea. The funerals of four German airmen who were killed in an air battle two days ago were taking place during yesterday's air battle." (This statement is not quite correct. The enemy aircraft seen to explode in the air was actually the collision between Mick and the Me. 110, but as it happened at about 27,000 feet the onlookers on the ground naturally could not see exactly what occurred.)

★   ★   ★

The following day was rather cloudy and nothing very much happened except that we were bombed by a single Ju. 88 which came over under cover of cloud. Some Hurricanes were up after him and one of them sighted him when about five miles south of the aerodrome. A terrific chase ensued with the Hun dodging in and out of cloud and the Hurricane firing madly at him whenever he could see him. They passed right over our heads at about 1,000 feet; I had never heard a fighter's eight machine-guns firing before except when in the cockpit myself, when the noise is very muffled, and I was amazed! It's the most terrific, tearing, ripping sound, just like hundreds of girls ripping sheets of calico. I must say this Hun pilot was very cool, because, despite the Hurricane on his tail, he still did his run-up towards his target and let go four big bombs. They fell just beyond our mess, made four huge craters in a field, shook everybody in the mess, but did no damage whatsoever. A very lucky escape.

Novi got so excited when the Hurricane started firing that he jumped up on to some sandbags and shouted at the top of his voice to the Hurricane, "Shoot, shoot!" The Junkers got back into cloud again before the Hurricane could shoot him down, but he had to land about twenty miles away as one of the Hurricane's bullets had hit an oil pipe. So we got him after all.

Just about this time Michael made a joke which I think is worth recording. We pilot officers are not exactly over-paid for our services, and Michael suggested the following variation of Mr. Churchill's now famous phrase — "Never in the history of human conflict has so much been owed by so many to so few — for so little."

Monday, 30th September, was a very eventful day for me and easily the most successful that I had experienced. The weather was brilliantly clear, and when we got up we shook our heads dismally, as we knew there would be a lot of trouble. As Mac used to remark, "We should have quite a job to keep the Grim Reaper at bay."

We arrived down at our aircraft about 7.30a.m., and I walked over to my Spitfire, as I always did first thing every morning, and checked over everything in the cockpit with the utmost care, because if later we got any orders to "scramble" we always had to get off the ground in such a hurry that we had no time to look at anything.

So I checked over the whole machine carefully, looked at the petrol gauges and turned on the petrol, checked that the mixture control was in "rich" and the airscrew in fine pitch, set the elevator trim, opened the radiator, turned on the oxygen, and checked it, switched on the reflector sights, checked the air pressure for the gun system, and switched on the camera gun. Everything was perfect, as indeed it always was. I walked back to the hut, put on my Mae West, and started to write up this diary, my daily occupation.

All the rest of the squadron who happened to be on duty were down there too, twelve of us in all, some writing or reading, some asleep, and the rest playing cards. Thus we spent the war.

Soon after 10.30a.m. we heard the telephone bell ring in the next room, and the telephone orderly ran to our door and yelled in his usual stentorian voice, "Squadron take off, patrol 25,000 feet". I threw this diary into a chair, the card players dropped their hands, and everybody sprinted out of the door towards their machines. All the airmen were running hard too, and by the time I got to my Spitfire two men were already there to help me on with my parachute and then fasten my harness when I was in the cockpit. I put on the starter and ignition switches, turned on the R.T., gave the priming pump a couple of strokes, and pressed the starter button. The engine started immediately, and I put on my helmet and oxygen mask, and within ninety seconds of the alarm coming through we were all taxi-ing out on the aerodrome. I was leading Green Section with Novi and Johnny behind me, and we got out to our taking-off point and turned into wind. I looked round at Novi and he gave me "thumbs up", meaning all O.K., and Johnny did likewise. I dropped my hand, opened the throttle and we all accelerated rapidly over the aerodrome and took off. The rest of the squadron were either taking off or already in the air, and we all joined up and started to climb towards Swanage, nearly fifty miles away.

I used to love flying with the squadron like this. It was always a grand sight to see twelve Spitfires sweeping along together in formation — twelve pilots, fifteen thousand horsepower, and ninety-six machine-guns with a total fire power of 120,000 rounds a minute. Altogether quite a formidable proposition!

102

A few minutes later the Controller in the Operations Room called us up on the R.T. "Hallo, Blue Leader, more than 100 enemy aircraft now approaching Swanage, height 20,000 feet." The C.O. replied immediately, "Blue Leader answering, your message received and understood."

We continued to climb — 10,000 feet, 15,000, 20,000, 25,000 feet, and as we got higher, I kept turning on more oxygen for myself and every few moments looking at the dashboard to check the oil pressure, and temperature, radiator temperature, boost pressure, and oxygen delivery. Everything was running like clockwork, always very reassuring when you know that a big fight is imminent.

We were now high over Dorset, nearly 27,000 feet, and rapidly approaching Swanage, when somebody called up on the R.T., "Enemy ahead on the left". I looked round and saw a long way in the distance a big formation of enemy fighters circling over the coast. I don't think there were any bombers on this occasion; it was just a very strong fighter patrol sent over to annoy us and destroy as many of our fighters as possible.

Frank (who was leading us that day, as the C.O. was ill) altered direction slightly and we flew right out into Weymouth Bay and then turned in towards land again, so as to approach the enemy from the sun. This was a clever move, as it turned out.

It was now obviously a matter of moments only before we were in the thick of it. I turned my trigger on to "Fire", increased the engine revs. to 3,000 r.p.m. by slipping the constant speed control fully forward, and

103

"pulled the plug", i.e. pushed the small handle on the throttle quadrant that cuts out the automatic boost control thus allowing one to use emergency full power.

A few seconds later, about six Me. 109s flew across right in front of us. I don't think they saw us till too late as we were coming out of the sun. Michael was leading Blue Section and I was leading Green, and immediately we swung our sections round and turned on to the tails of the enemy. They then saw us — too late — and tried to escape by diving.

We all went down after them in one glorious rush and I saw Michael, who was about a hundred yards ahead of me, open fire at the last Messerschmidt in the enemy line. A few seconds later, this machine more or less fell to pieces in mid-air — some very nice shooting on Michael's part. I distinctly remember him saying on the R.T., "That's got you, you bastard," though he never recollects it!

The victim that I had selected for myself was about 500 yards ahead of me, and still diving hard at very high speed. God, what a dive that was! I came down on full throttle from 27,000 feet to 1,000 feet in a matter of a few seconds, and the speed rose with incredible swiftness — 400 m.p.h., 500, 550, 600 m.p.h. I never reached this speed before and probably never shall again. I have a sort of dim recollection of the sea coming up towards me at an incredible rate and also feeling an awful pain in my ears, though I was not really conscious of this in the heat of the moment. I pulled out of the dive as gently as I could, but the strain was terrific and there was a sort of black mist in front of my eyes, though I did not quite "black out".

The Messerschmidt was now just ahead of me. I came up behind him, and gave him a terrific burst of fire at very close range. The effect of a Spitfire's eight guns has to be seen to be believed. Hundreds of bullets poured into him and he rocked violently, then turned over on his back, burst into flames and dived straight down into the sea a few miles off Swanage. The pilot made no attempt to get out and was obviously dead.

I watched him hit the water in a great cloud of white foam, and then turned round to see what was going on.

A few of our Spitfires were chasing Messerschmidts all over the place and obviously a very nice little massacre was in progress, as a few seconds later I saw another Hun go into the sea. I then saw another Me. 109 going back to France as hard as he could and I chased after him, caught him fairly easily, and put a good burst into him. He swerved slightly, his cockpit covering broke off the machine and flew just past my head and he then dived steeply.

I waited to see him hit the water, but he was only shamming, as he flattened out again just above the sea, and continued full speed for home, though his machine was now smoking and obviously badly hit.

For the first time in this war, I felt a certain pity for this German pilot and was rather reluctant to finish him off. From the moment I saw him, he really had no chance of escape as my Spitfire was so much faster than his Messerschmidt, and the last few moments must have been absolute hell for him. I could almost feel his desperation as he made this last attempt to get away.

But if I let him go, he would come back to England another day and possibly shoot down some of our pilots. In the few seconds during which all this was happening, I did not consciously make these reflections; my blood was up anyway and I was very excited, but I distinctly remember feeling rather reluctant.

However, I caught him up again and made no mistake this time. I fired almost all my remaining ammunition at very close range, and he crashed into the sea, going at terrific speed, and disappeared immediately. I circled round the spot, but there was no trace of anything.

I now looked round and discovered that I could see the French coast clearly ahead and that I was only about fifteen miles from Cherbourg. England was nowhere to be seen.

In the excitement of the chase I had not realized how far we were going, and I turned round very hastily and started on my sixty-mile trip back to the English coast. It seemed to take a long time, and I was very relieved when, still a long way out to sea, I saw the white cliffs begin to appear ahead. One never knows what an engine may do after running it so long on absolutely full throttle and the idea of drowning out in mid-Channel never did appeal to me.

I was now feeling very happy and pleased with myself — I had always wanted to get two Huns in one fight. I approached the cliffs in Weymouth Bay, flying only a few feet over the water at nearly 300 m.p.h., and when I was almost hitting the cliff I pulled the stick back and rocketed over the top to the very considerable amazement of some soldiers who were on the other side. And so back home, flying very low the whole way, generally playing the fool and feeling gloriously happy and elated!

Everybody was safely back and we had destroyed five Messerschmidts — quite a nice morning's work.

In the afternoon there was another alarm at about 3.30p.m., and again we took off and made for the coast at Swanage, climbing all the time. We passed over Weymouth, and then turned round and approached Swanage down from the sun.

A few moments later we saw a few machines down on our left, which I thought were Hurricanes. However, Frank, who was leading the squadron, told me to take Green Section down to investigate, so three of us, Novi, Johnny, and I, broke away from the squadron, and dived down to the left. Unfortunately Johnny's engine was giving trouble, and he could not keep up with Novi and me, and got left a long way behind.

I was still under the impression that these machines were Hurricanes, but as we got nearer I recognized them as Me. 109s and shouted to Novi accordingly.

We both attacked together and he opened fire on the last one on the line and shot it down almost immediately. I don't think they ever saw us till we opened fire as we dived on them out of the sun.

They split up quickly and I went after one and gave him a quick deflection burst, which I don't think hit

107

him, but certainly startled him, as he promptly proceeded to take the most violent evasive tactics. For nearly two minutes we dived and zoomed and turned madly all over the sky in a desperate effort to get on each other's tails. It was just like the practice dog fights that Geoff and I used to have together, except that in this case the slightest mistake would probably cost the loser his life, instead of a pint of beer.

But the Spitfire is more manoeuvrable than the Messerschmidt, and I had no difficulty in keeping on his tail more or less, though he was sufficiently quick in his turns to prevent me getting my sights on him for more than a fraction of a second.

Finally, after a dive even faster than before, he zoomed up almost vertically for 2,000 feet, going straight into the sun in an effort to shake me off that way. Almost completely dazzled, I managed nevertheless to follow him up and when he did a stall turn at the top I got another quick burst at him without apparent effect.

At the top of the zoom I rolled over on to my back, but the recoil of the guns practically stalled me and I hung there for a second upside down and then fell away in a very drunken dive after the 109. He streaked away in front of me, going hard for a layer of cloud. I went down vertically after him, gathering speed like a bullet and doing a quick aileron turn to get into line again. Outside the cockpit I could see the earth and the clouds and the sky all apparently revolving crazily round my head, but they did so in a curiously detached way because I was conscious only of the small racing object in front.

He managed to reach the cloud below and I chased after him, missed him with another burst, and then hunted him through this cloud for some miles, dodging in and out, and seeing him for a fleeting instant every now and then.

He wasn't very clever about this, and he never changed course in the cloud, and thus, if I lost him, I had only to keep straight on and I would pick him up again.

We tore over Weymouth, going very fast indeed, and passed out to sea. This was his undoing, as he probably thought he had shaken me off and he made the bad mistake of climbing out of the cloud. I climbed up behind, came into very close range, and then absolutely blasted him. He turned over, and spun down into the cloud, streaming glycol smoke, which meant that his radiator had been hit. I dived below cloud but could see no trace of him at all, and I think there can be very little doubt that he crashed into the sea, as he was badly hit and certainly could not have reached France with a radiator leaking like that. But I had not seen him actually crash, and therefore could only claim him as a "probable".

My camera gun film showed later that I had him for several seconds in the middle of my sights at very close range, so I don't think he could possibly have survived.

I hung round for a few minutes but saw no other Huns and returned home. The rest of the squadron had not been in action, and so Novi and I were the only lucky ones. He had shot down two of the Me. 109s, and the pilot got out of the second machine and tried to open his parachute. One of the rigging lines fouled it however, and it only opened slightly, and the unfortunate German therefore continued his drop with scarcely any reduction in speed, and was killed.

Novi, bloodthirsty as ever where Germans are concerned, recounted this story to us with great relish and a wealth of very descriptive gestures.

This had been a good day for B Flight, and we all felt in very good form that evening. Michael, Noel, Johnny, and I went over to Winchester and had dinner with the Berrys. We had a very amusing evening together; Major Berry stood us all some champagne and we returned home taking a distinctly rosy view of life. It was one of the best days I ever had in the squadron.

And thus ended that eventful month, September 1940.

OCTOBER–NOVEMBER

In the first few days of October, to our very real regret, the news came through that the C.O. was leaving us. He had been promoted Wing Commander and was going to command another station.

We were all delighted to hear, just before he left, that he had been awarded the D.S.O.

We expected that Frank, A Flight Commander, would take command of the squadron, and certainly it would have been a very good thing, because in the C.O.'s absence he always led us so well that everybody had complete confidence in him.

However, the powers that be decreed otherwise, and we got instead Squadron Leader R., who proved to be a very good C.O. and an excellent leader. He was the pilot who, about two months before, shot down two Me. 109s, and having finished his ammunition, saw a third 109 and chased it for forty miles, and finally so frightened the German pilot by making dummy attacks at him, that he landed in a field and was captured. The C.O. then threw him a packet of Players, waved, and the German waved back, and then he flew off. A very cool bit of work!

We had a terrific farewell party the night before the C.O. left. Pamela and Maurice came over for the early part of the evening, and we all adjourned to the Square Club. We then came back for dinner in the mess and went down to the C.O.'s house, where a large barrel of beer had been specially installed for the occasion, and a very good and rather rowdy time was had by all.

The next morning the C.O. came down and bade us all goodbye and good luck, and said how proud he had been to command such a grand squadron. He stood there, looking exactly like a rather sheepish schoolboy, while we all sang "For he's a jolly good fellow" at the top of our voices, and then he drove off.

That afternoon we took off to do some practice flying, and when we came in to land again and put our undercarriages down, only one of Novi's wheels would come down and the other remained locked obstinately in the raised position. Try as he would he was unable to move it. This meant that it was very dangerous to land, as one wheel would hit the ground and the Spitfire — still doing about 75 m.p.h. — would then somersault towards the missing wheel. I called him up on the R.T. and told him that he must not land but instead climb up and bale out.

I was flying very close to him and we climbed up to 5,000 feet over Salisbury Plain, and then Novi opened his sliding hood, took off his helmet, undid his harness and prepared to abandon ship. However, he seemed to experience some difficulty in getting out of the cockpit into the slipstream, and finally he turned the machine over on to its back and dropped neatly out of his seat.

The Spitfire promptly dived into the corner of a small wood and burst into flames. Novi, after fumbling for his release cord, opened his parachute, and a few minutes later he dropped into the middle of a hen run, to the consternation of the poultry.

People seemed to spring up from all over the place and rush towards him, and so I circled the spot for a few minutes, as I thought that, with his rather broken English, he might be mistaken for a German parachutist. But everything was O.K. We sent out a car to collect him, and half an hour later he was in the mess again, none the worse for his experience except for a bruised arm. The machine that he had been flying was not a very good one — it was rather old and slower than the new ones — so we were all very grateful to him for writing it off!

The following day, 6th October, was misty and rainy and we sat in the mess, read the papers, and had a beer before lunch. The weather seemed so thick that obviously no Hun would get over — or so we thought.

However, at about 12.30p.m. the loudspeakers announced that an enemy aircraft was approaching us in the clouds. We could do nothing about it, as we could not possibly intercept him in such weather, so we ordered another beer apiece and were rather amused by the whole business.

A few seconds later we all heard a very sharp whistle, and everybody in the mess — about thirty people in all, lounging in armchairs and reading the papers — suddenly threw themselves with astonishing agility on to the floor. I remember that Michael and I met with a crash under the table and spilt all the beer, while our Intelligence Officer, McK., who is too fat to get underneath anything, merely lay hopefully on his back.

There were two big flashes outside the window, and two terrific explosions that seemed to rock the whole building to its foundations. We cowered and waited expectantly for the next, but nothing happened and we rose cautiously to our feet.

No windows were broken (except one in the billiard room, where Johnny was just playing a shot as the bomb dropped, and he was so surprised that he slung his cue through the window).

The bombs had fallen in a field just in front of the mess. We walked over to inspect the craters, picked up a few splinters and wandered back and ordered more beer before lunch, to replace that spilt in the rapid dive on to the floor.

The following day, Monday, 7th October, dawned very bright and clear, and we expected trouble from the moment we got up.

But nothing happened till about 5.30p.m., when we were ordered off to patrol Weymouth at a height of 25,000 feet. We took off and climbed up steadily in a south-westerly direction, trying to get as much height as possible before reaching the coast.

I don't think I have ever seen such a clear day in my life. From 15,000 feet I could see Plymouth and far beyond into Cornwall; up in the north the whole coast of South Wales was clearly visible, from the Severn at Gloucester and away beyond Swansea in the west, while on our left, to the south, the Channel glistened and sparkled in the sun, and the French coast and the Channel Islands, although seventy-five miles away, seemed to be just under my wing-tip.

But I can't say that I appreciated this superb view very much under the circumstances, because I was busily engaged behind the squadron, anxiously scanning the sky for the Messerschmidts which we knew would soon be arriving.

The sun was so brilliant and dazzling that it was very difficult to see anything clearly in the glare, and yet this made it even more important to maintain the utmost vigilance, as the Me. 109s are very good at jumping on one out of the sun.

When we were almost at Weymouth, at about 20,000 feet, we saw an enemy bomber formation some miles out to sea, and at the same moment, various people saw a lot of Me. 109s above us, apparently about to dive down and attack us. About four people at once started to shout warnings on the R.T. and there was a perfect babel of excited voices, which rather added to the confusion.

B Flight was rather behind A Flight, and we started to break up, as it is quite hopeless to watch enemy aircraft above and behind, and at the same time keep in formation with the rest of the squadron.

I hardly saw anybody again for the rest of the action, and most of us never engaged at all. Several of us continued to patrol for about half an hour, by which time the whole affair was obviously over and Operations Room told us to land. When we got back we found that A Flight had been rather more successful.

Being in front of us and therefore to some extent guarded by us, they managed to keep together, and they attacked a formation of Me. 110s and destroyed five or six of them. We now had a very anxious half-hour, as four pilots were still missing. However, some news soon started to come through — John's machine had been hit by a cannon shell from an Me. 110 which came up behind him as he was engaged in shooting down an Me. 109. The shell burst in the wing, and put a lot of little splinters into his side, but he wasn't badly hurt and landed safely and returned to us the next day. Mike got a bullet in his leg, and baled out and landed near Blandford, where they took him to hospital, and he was O.K., though with a rather big hole in his leg.

Frank shot down an Me. 110 in flames, but the rear-gunner managed to hit Frank's engine and he had to land in a field.

Within two minutes a crowd of people had sprung up from an apparently deserted countryside, and offered him cups of tea and coffee. The police and soldiers then arrived on the scene, and had a great argument as to who should give him a party that night. The police won, and bore Frank off in triumph to the local pub, where the police and the inhabitants plied him (and themselves) with pints of beer for four solid hours and then drove him back and delivered him into the mess in a distinctly intoxicated condition.

Well, that was three out of the four safe, but Sergeant F. was still missing. We waited for some hours, hoping to hear that he had landed somewhere, but later that evening somebody rang up to say that his body had been found. He was last seen by us when attacking the Me. 110s, and his machine must have been hit, because a number of men saw his Spitfire spinning down from a great height.

He recovered from the spin, got into another one, recovered again, spun again and then apparently decided to get out. But he had left it too late, because his parachute did not have time to open properly and he was killed by the fall. He had not been hit at all and if only he hadn't stayed so long in the damaged machine he would almost certainly have got away with it.

A great pity, as he was a very good and resolute pilot, and had been all through the summer's fighting.

Weymouth certainly seemed to be an unlucky spot for 609. Apart from the Dunkirk casualties, we lost eight pilots during the summer, and seven of these — Peter, Pip, Gordon, Buck, G., Mick, and Sergeant F. were all killed in the south-west.

Only Geoff was killed near London, and when one considers how much fighting we did both in the London and Southampton areas, it does seem curious that all our losses should occur in one place.

[By a very tragic coincidence, on the afternoon that this paragraph was written, 28th November, both John and B. were killed over the Isle of Wight during a raid into Southampton. The last heard of John was when he called up on the R.T. and said that he had shot down an Me. 109. He never came back and a few days later the German Official Communiqué said that one of their most successful fighter pilots, Major Wieck, had been shot down by an English fighter near the Isle of Wight, and that the English machine itself was immediately shot down by another member of the German formation. As no English pilots claimed any victims in this fight, Major Wieck must have been the Messerschmidt pilot that John spoke about on the R.T., and this has since been confirmed by the Air Ministry.

B. also just disappeared, and two months later, in January, Berlin sent a telegram to the Air Ministry via Geneva, saying that his body had been washed ashore at Boulogne and buried there.

John was the most successful pilot in the squadron and an exceptionally good fighter pilot. He was given a bar to his D.F.C. shortly after his death, and I don't think an award was ever better deserved. He possessed also a brilliant intellect and was a well-known journalist on the *Yorkshire Post*.

I did not know B. so well, as he had not been in the squadron for long, but I liked him and the loss of these two was a big shock to everybody.]

A few days later I got five days' leave and again flew to Peterborough and caught the train north from there. Dorothy and I spent a very happy few days at home. As usual, I caught the afternoon train from Wakefield and arrived in London nearly two hours late, as there was a big raid in progress. It was almost impossible to get a taxi at King's Cross, but finally about six of us crowded into one, and drove through the dark and deserted streets to Piccadilly. There was a lot of gunfire, and every now and then the deep "whoom" of a bursting bomb could be heard.

I walked round to the Trocadero and had some dinner and then met an amusing Canadian soldier (I always seemed to met Canadians on my evenings in town). We had a few beers together, and then decided that we could do with some bacon and eggs. It was just about midnight and we walked round to Lyons' Corner House in Coventry Street, and ordered our food. We had just started our meal when there was a terrible crash outside — all the glass in the windows fell in and the whole building seemed to rock to its foundations.

I was amazed by the complete lack of any panic or confusion; most people just looked up for a moment and then resumed their conversation again.

A few minutes later we went outside and found that the bomb had fallen just on the other side of the road next to the Prince of Wales Theatre. Very little structural damage had been done as it exploded in a small open space, but there was hardly a window left in the whole of Coventry Street.

The pavements were almost ankle deep in broken glass, and a large squad of men were just assembling to start the job of clearing it all up.

A few moments later I bade my Canadian friend good-night, and went back to bed at the hotel. There was no further excitement that night.

When I got back to the squadron I found that very little had happened in my absence, and for the next few days life continued to be very quiet. However, the weather improved slowly, and a few days later we were sitting down near the aircraft when the order came through to take off. We all got off the ground and started to climb towards the coast. At about 10,000 feet there was some cloud, and as soon as we got above this I looked round and above, and saw many thousands of feet above us at least thirty Messerschmidt 110s, accompanied by a lot of Me. 109s. At first I thought they were our own fighters and called up to the C.O. and suggested that they were some Hurricanes. The C.O. took one look and replied, "No, they must be Huns." And so they were, as I recognized a moment later.

We were in a hopeless position, a long way below them and outlined against the white cloud underneath us. However, we continued to climb, in the hope of somehow managing to get in one attack, and all the time we watched the Messerschmidts like cats, as sooner or later they would obviously drop down on us. Altogether rather an unpleasant few minutes.

It was very difficult watching them, as they were almost in the sun, and the glare was awful.

Suddenly I saw two Me. 109s just behind John's Spitfire. How they got there I don't know — I never saw them come down and nobody else did either. They must have dived very fast indeed, and they had just opened fire when I saw them. I remember distinctly their yellow noses and the white streaks caused by their cannon shells.

I immediately shouted on the R.T., "Look out, Messerschmidts, they're coming down". I have never seen the squadron break up so quickly. The machines turned sharply away in all directions and dived hard for the cloud. I went down with everybody else, pulled out after a few thousand feet and looked round. Apart from a few Spitfires dashing around, there was nothing to be seen. We all waited a little longer, but met no more enemy, and soon afterwards we were ordered to land. And so a lot of very angry pilots returned home.

Nobody was missing and John was quite O.K., though there were one or two bullet holes in his wings. Those Me. 109 pilots must have been bad shots; if any of us had fired at them in similar circumstances they wouldn't have got away.

And there was more good news. We had shot down a couple of Me. 109s, though it seemed incredible when we were at such a disadvantage. When the squadron broke up and dived away, both Noel and Novi stayed up there with the Me. 109s — a very cool and risky thing to do, since they were in such a hopeless position. However, like some other audacious schemes, it worked.

Noel was just turning round when a bullet crashed through his cockpit roof three inches above his head, and several more hit his machine. He whipped round and saw two 109s calmly flying away and not paying the slightest attention to him — perhaps they thought they had shot him down. So he caught them up and shot down the rear one.

Novi was also attacked, but managed to shoot down another 109, which crashed near Bournemouth. When the machine was near the ground, the pilot got out and just managed to open his parachute in time, but landed

121

very heavily and lay on the ground, probably winded by the fall. Novi circled round and said afterwards, in his rather broken English, "I circle round, bloddy German lies down, he is dead, O.K. But I look again, he is now sitting up, no bloddy good." He was very disappointed; in his opinion the only good Germans are dead Germans.

After this little affair the bad weather set in again and we did very little for the next few weeks. After the long strain of the summer and autumn, when we hardly ever got out in the evening, as we were on duty till dark, the reaction now began to set in, and we seemed to go out on parties nearly every night.

On Thursday, 17th October, after an uneventful and rainy day, we came into the mess for tea and I got a plate and settled down in a chair to read the paper. A few minutes later the C.O. came up to me and put something on the paper with the remark, "Look what the post has just brought for you".

It was the D.F.C. ribbon!

I was so surprised that I just stared at it for a moment without grasping what it meant. I remember getting to my feet, still rather dazed and being congratulated by various people.

Johnny had got one also, and he soon produced a needle and thread and sewed his on. I took mine to my batman to fix it on my tunic, and then walked downstairs again feeling better than I'd ever felt before.

We had the most terrific party that night and, I should imagine, consumed most of the mess stock of Pimms. Altogether a riotous evening!

★   ★   ★

122

In the action on 7th October, in which Sergeant F. was killed and Mike wounded, we had brought our score of Huns definitely destroyed to ninety-nine, and as we seemed to get some fight every few days it looked as though we should complete our century very quickly. But, unfortunately, the German Air Force did not seem very keen to offer themselves up for the slaughter, and so we waited impatiently for over a fortnight, hoping every day that our luck would change. No batsman, hovering on the edge of his century, was ever more keen than we were to see the 100 up. But after the murderous losses inflicted on them in the previous two months, the Germans had reduced their daylight bombing activity practically to nil, and nothing seemed to come our way.

However, on Monday, 21st October, our chance arrived. The day was cloudy — ideal conditions for single bombers to carry out hit-and-run raids, and about 12.30p.m. a Junkers 88 appeared out of the clouds and bombed a place in the Midlands. He then turned south again towards the coast at Bournemouth, on his way home, flying very low the whole way so as to escape detection by any of our fighters who might be above.

Two of our people, Frank and Sidney, were up after him and were waiting near the coast to try to intercept him on his way out. A few moments later Operations Room called them up on the R.T. and said, "He should be near you now, flying very low".

A second later they saw him practically underneath — a very nice bit of work on the part of Ops.

123

They both dived down to attack and Frank went in first, opened fire at very close range, and damaged an engine badly. It must have been an exciting chase, as the Ju. 88 was going down below the level of the trees in his desperate efforts to escape.

Frank then broke away, and Sidney opened fire, and almost immediately the Hun dived into a field. There was a terrific explosion and the wreckage was scattered over four fields. All the crew were killed instantly.

And that was that. There was great rejoicing at the aerodrome when the news came through a few minutes later, and a considerable party was organized for that night.

About 6.30p.m. we trooped into the writing-room and there found a couple of waiters behind the bar and almost hidden by the large stock of champagne and brandy that had been installed for the occasion. A satisfactory if somewhat boozy party ensued; everybody was in top form and we all felt distinctly pleased with ourselves and life generally. We drank to the C.O., we drank to the Poles, we drank to the squadron, and in fact we toasted practically everything we could think of, in round after round of champagne cocktails.

It was a very good party.

A day or two later I flew to Wales to pick up a little aeroplane belonging to the C.O., as he wanted to have it in the squadron. I flew over with Ogle in the Harvard and we landed and went over to the hangar where the Drone was kept. I was amazed when I saw it!

It is a tiny single-seater aeroplane with a 10 h.p. Ford engine, and when we started it up it sounded like a motorcycle.

I didn't see how I could possibly fly over 120 miles in it. Ogle went back in the Harvard, having made several very gloomy jokes about my chances of survival, and I took off in the Drone. Its top speed was about 45 m.p.h. and it had a very slow rate of climb, so that if I saw a hill about two miles ahead, I had to start climbing immediately in order to get over the top. A great change from a Spitfire!

I flew round Cardiff and then along the flat stretch of coast towards Newport, and when the river became fairly narrow I crossed over and skirted round the north of Bristol and then down towards home. I hardly ever went above 200 feet and caused a great sensation as I floated gently over the countryside, past farms and villages where I could see everybody running out to look at this strange craft. It was a lovely day and I thoroughly enjoyed my gentle "stroll" over such grand country.

I remember that near Warminster I joined up with a large flock of starlings that were going my way, and we all flew along together for some miles, after which I throttled back a little and let them race on ahead. And coming along a road over the Plain I met a convoy of Army lorries, crowded with troops, all going in the same direction as me and approximately at the same speed, so I flew along with them and so close that I could have practically reached out and shaken hands with them. They were highly amused and waved back hard.

I arrived safely home amidst great hilarity and many ribald remarks. The trip had taken two and a half hours and I used four and a half gallons of petrol. I think it was one of the most enjoyable flights I have had.

A day or two after this I went home on leave from the 24th to the 29th October. We had a very pleasant though quiet time and Dorothy and I went to see various people and altogether enjoyed the few days.

On the 29th I returned to the squadron for the official centenary party, the other one apparently having been unofficial, though nobody would have noticed it.

Quite a lot of people came down — Air Marshal Barrett, Sir Quintin Brand, Air Commodore Peake, who was the first C.O. of the squadron in the days at Yeadon before the war, and, to our intense pleasure, our old C.O., Wing Commander D., D.S.O. Also various Guardees came up from Camberley, and Michael and I took off in a couple of Spitfires and did a little formation flying and a few upward rolls for their benefit.

And so on to the party. Great quantities of champagne were consumed; we had an excellent dinner and some speeches, including one from D., which we all cheered to the echo.

It was fitting that he should be there — under his command we had come through the summer campaign of 1940 with as fine a record as any squadron in the

R.A.F., and this dinner, besides celebrating our century, was also celebrating a very successful few months' fighting.

The actual score was 100 enemy aircraft definitely destroyed, a big number probably destroyed, and many more damaged.

This meant a loss of about 800 German airmen killed or captured, and against this our own losses were thirteen pilots killed.[1]

Sir Quintin Brand also congratulated us and said that whenever he was in the Operations Room at Group during a raid and he heard that 609 had

---

[1] The following report appeared in the *Yorkshire Post*: "A Yorkshire Auxiliary Air Force fighter squadron has shot down 100 enemy planes, states the Air Ministry News Service. The 100th victim was a Junkers 88 bomber, which was sent plunging earthwards over the South Coast.

"The squadron has fought with distinction at Dunkirk, in the Channel battles, and in the defence of London and the cities of the South and West. Over Dunkirk, nine of the Spitfires shot down in one day four bombers and two Messerschmidt 109s.

"One day, near Portland, within the space of a few minutes, they shot down nine Junkers 87 dive-bombers and four Messerschmidt 109s. This victory was achieved without loss.

"During the first big raid on London the pilots shot down two Messerschmidt 110s, a Dornier 17, and a Messerschmidt 109 — again without loss.

"One of the pilots, when over Southampton, was the first to attack a formation of 70 bombers. At the end of half an hour the raiders had been driven off with the loss of 15 bombers and 16 fighters."

intercepted the enemy, then he knew that lots of Huns would be shot down at little or no cost to ourselves.

Just about this time a very unusual occurrence took place in our area, and though it had nothing whatever to do with the squadron, I think it is worth recording.

Early one morning four German airmen walked into a village near Shaftesbury in Dorset and gave themselves up. The aeroplane in which presumably they must have come down could not be found anywhere. At about the same time a Dornier bomber made a perfect landing (without undercarriage) on the mud flats at Ipswich nearly 130 miles away.

There was no crew in the Dornier and they could not be found. So everybody at Ipswich was saying, "Where are the crew for this aeroplane?" and everybody at Shaftesbury was saying, "Where is the aeroplane for this crew?" The puzzle was soon solved, but it is an amazing story.

The bomber had left its base near Cherbourg en route for a raid on Liverpool and was flying up the west country in very bad weather when it ran into a heavy electrical storm near Shrewsbury. The machine was damaged by the storm and the pilot decided to abandon the raid and go home again. So he turned about and flew south, but somewhere in Somerset he ran into another storm with a heavy electric discharge, and this completely upset their compass. They continued on their course, crossed the Channel and arrived safely over the French coast — almost home. They then noticed that according to their compass they were steering due north, and obviously this is not the direction to fly if you want to get from England to France. So they turned back again and flew "south" on their compass, crossed the Channel again, and saw the English coast beneath. Obviously, they thought this was the French coast, as they had flown south for so long, and as they could not find an aerodrome and were getting short of petrol, they baled out and walked to the nearest village to get help.

They were quite convinced that they were in France, and one can imagine their mortification at finding themselves prisoners of war, particularly as they had already got home safely and then turned back again over enemy territory.

I bet they cursed that compass! Anyway, to finish the story, the bomber flew along on its automatic pilot (or George), and when the petrol ran out, it landed safely at Ipswich.

This story is amazing, but absolutely true.

At the beginning of November the weather improved again and became brilliantly clear and cold, and the enemy took advantage of this weather and sent in some very strong fighter patrols towards Southampton and Portsmouth. They came over at immense heights, anything up to 35,000 feet, and were planned with the sole intention of annoying us and killing as many of us as possible.

No bombs were dropped and they were merely offensive fighter patrols.

They certainly did annoy us, and particularly so because we had not time to get up to their height. So we flew about at 30,000 feet, all the time watching in painful suspense those blasted little Me. 109s playing about above us.

This sort of thing happened on several occasions at the beginning of November, and though we did not have anybody killed, I think we were very lucky to get away with it. Fortunately the German pilots showed very little determination to press home their advantage — if we ever got them in a similar position they would have regretted it bitterly.

On 1st November we took off to intercept a large enemy fighter patrol coming in towards Southampton. On this occasion we were trying to fly together with a Hurricane squadron, as we thought that if we went out in larger numbers it might make up for our disadvantage in height. But we found it rather difficult to keep in formation with them, as we were so much faster than their Hurricanes, so we passed underneath them and started to draw ahead.

Operations Room now called us up and said that we were very near the enemy. We all strained our eyes, but could see nothing at all; by this time we were up at 32,000 feet and at that height the sky is a very deep blue, and the glare of the sun is so strong that it completely dazzles you if you look anywhere near it. Add to this the fact that owing to the intense cold our breath was condensing on the inside of the cockpit covering and freezing so that it looked exactly like frosted glass, and you can imagine that we could

130

scarcely see out at all. Not very pleasant when you know that at any moment a lot of Me. 109s may be dropping down on you from out of the sun, just like a ton of bricks. Suddenly Novi let out a yell and we all turned round and saw the Hurricanes behind us diving away in all directions, while about four Me. 109s, very conspicuous by their bright yellow noses, were climbing up rapidly into the blue again after their lightning attack. Obviously the Hurricanes had been caught by surprise, and we heard later that three of them had been shot down, though only one of the pilots was killed.

We were very glad that we had decided to overtake them or we should have been the rear squadron and caught it instead.

Altogether these affairs were not very pleasant as we could never even relieve our feelings by letting off a few rounds at the Me. 109s, since they were always so far above us.

The next day one section was ordered to take off and patrol Lyme Bay (just west of Weymouth) as a single enemy aircraft was approaching the coast. I took off, leading Green Section, and we went hard for Weymouth at about 15,000 feet. We arrived over Lyme Bay and circled round, when Zura shouted that he had seen a machine below. The Poles always seemed to see things first — they had marvellous eyes and knew how to use them. So we dived after this machine on full throttle and started to overtake him very rapidly. As we got closer, I saw that it was a large four-engined bomber; we knew that the Germans had some because

131

they had been used occasionally against this country, but nobody had ever succeeded in shooting one down.

I was very excited, for I was quite certain that we were going to be the first people in the R.A.F. to achieve this distinction. We were now in range, and I was just about to open fire and let him have it, when Hank, who was flying No. 2, shouted, "I think it's one of ours." I took my thumb off the trigger and flew alongside, though keeping out of range in case he should be hostile. To my amazement there were the red and blue roundels on the side — it was a Stirling. It was a good thing that Hank stopped me, because I was just about to fire and we should not have been very popular if we had destroyed one of our latest and largest bombers. Though it wouldn't have been our fault, as he had no business at all to be flying around the coast like that, and Operations Room had told us definitely that he was hostile. Anyway, all's well that ends well.

That night I woke up in the early hours and listened very sleepily to the steady drone of a German bomber somewhere above us. This continued for a few minutes, and then suddenly there was a very sharp hiss, followed by a thud and the tinkle of something breaking.

It sounded very close, far too close for my liking, and I got up and went out into the corridor, where I found everybody else had been wakened also and had got up to make inquiries. Everybody, that is, except Michael, who had been fairly well bombed in London and was so bored by these proceedings in the middle of the night that he stayed in bed. Well, we found that a 250-lb. delayed-action bomb had missed our wing in the mess by about forty yards, and had buried itself under the road. It was far too close to the mess for our liking, and it was a good job that it hadn't gone off.

We went to sleep on the other side of the building — all except Michael, who sleepily announced that he intended to stay where he was, and b— the bomb anyway.

We had some more fun with the bomb later.

November 8th was certainly one of the outstanding days of my life, though in the morning it seemed to be a very normal one.

For the last fortnight I had been ringing up Dorothy every night and inquiring anxiously if young Nicholas was showing any signs of making his appearance in this world.

He was due any time after the first days of November, but had apparently decided that there was no hurry, and poor Dorothy used to announce sorrowfully every night that nothing had happened yet. So we waited in hope.

Down at the squadron everything was very quiet in the morning and we sat and generally idled the time away till lunch. About 3.30p.m. the Adjutant rang me up and said, "Do you know that you have been posted to Central Flying School for an instructor's course?"

This news staggered me, although I had known for the past week that it was a possibility, and the thought of leaving the squadron and all that grand crowd of people depressed me beyond words.

About half an hour later an alarm came through and we all took off and made for Southampton. This was my last flight with the squadron, and, by a curious coincidence, as both the C.O. and Frank were away, I led the squadron. I think I would have given ten years of my life then to be able to meet some Huns and have a really good and successful fight. It would have been a glorious finish to my career in 609 to have led them in such an affair. But alas, these last appearances are never as satisfactory as one could wish, and after about ten minutes' flight we were ordered to land again. The enemy must have already turned back for France.

We returned to the aerodrome and I ordered the sections to land, while I stayed up for a few minutes on my own. I knew that this was my last flight in my beloved Spitfire and I could not bring myself to land again and bid her farewell.

I climbed up to about 7,000 feet and came down in a long steep dive at nearly 500 m.p.h., and then went rocketing up again into an upward roll.

Up she went, round and up, with a great surge of power, just like the beautiful little thoroughbred that she was. And thus I bade farewell to my faithful companion of so many exciting days.

Half an hour later I walked into the mess and found a telegram waiting for me — "Dorothy fine son, everything O.K., congratulations". So Nicholas had arrived at last!

All my depression suddenly vanished and I felt better and happier than I'd ever felt before.

We had a terrific celebration party that night, firstly to greet the arrival of young Nicholas and secondly as my farewell to the squadron. Round after round of Pimms came up with almost monotonous regularity, and after dinner a very uproarious crowd sallied forth from the mess to go to the sergeants' dance. On the way over we decided to have a look at the bomb, which was still lying under the road, though a hole had been dug down to it. The tarpaulin that covered the hole was dragged off and we proceeded to hurl beer bottles at the bomb. Several direct hits were scored, and then Michael crawled down amid cheers of encouragement and duly spat on the end of the bomb, after which we felt that honour was satisfied, and we continued on our way to the dance.

Next morning I got up in very good time, as I intended flying up to Huddersfield that day. Unfortunately, however, the weather was very bad and visibility practically nil, so I had to wait all day. In the afternoon I had my portrait done by Captain Orde, who was going round all the fighter squadrons drawing various pilots on behalf of the Air Ministry. That evening we went and had dinner at the White Hart, and early next morning I jumped out of bed and looked at the weather. It was clear at last.

So I dressed hurriedly, had breakfast, said goodbye to everybody, and took off in the Harvard for my journey north.

How I hated leaving the squadron. For two and a half years I had been in 609, starting with those grand week-ends at Yeadon before the war, and the annual summer camp at Thorney Island or Church Fenton.

Looking back now, I see those glorious days as though outlined against a rapidly darkening background, because out of the gay and light-hearted company of friends who flew together at Church Fenton in August 1939, more than half were killed within twelve months.

But in those days none of us dreamt — or cared, I think, what lay ahead.

And what memories I have of 609 at war and in action; starting with that memorable patrol over France and the unpleasant suspense of the day at Hawkinge; Peter's death at Weymouth, and my first sight of the enemy, with the olive-green colour of the Junkers 87 and the red flashes of my guns seen against the dark evening sky; the never-to-be-forgotten moment when the enemy machine burst into flames under my fire and plunged straight down into the sea many thousands of feet below; the moment on the steps of the mess when I heard that Pip and Gordon had been killed that morning, and I felt so stunned that I could hardly think; our best fight of the war on 18th August, when we destroyed thirteen Huns in four minutes' fighting; the terrific battles over London in September and the spectacle of those enormous German formations droning steadily on, despite the hail of fire to which they were subjected; that terrible minute when I walked into Glenwood on 16th September and heard that Geoff was missing; ten days later, flying home for his funeral and arriving late despite all my efforts; diving down just behind Mick to attack a German formation, and seeing him collide head-on with a Messerschmidt at 26,000 feet over Swanage; that glorious swoop at 600 m.p.h. to catch a diving Me. 109 on 30th September, and a few minutes later, feeling rather sorry as I shot down another Me. 109 into the sea, so many miles from land; the suspense before we reached our 100 and the terrific celebrations that attended it; and the C.O. walking up to me and throwing the D.F.C. ribbon on my newspaper.

And then, too, there were the good friends I was leaving in the squadron; Michael, who had been my constant and amusing companion for the last eighteen months, Noel and Johnny (the former has since been killed in the Middle East and Johnny was lost over the Channel in 1941), Frank, Teeny, Bishop, Novi, and Osti. We had been through so much together and had such good times.

And I remembered, too, the gallant friends who had died during this epic summer: Geoff, Gordon, Pip, and all the others. How terrible, I thought, how terrible and how useless, that the cream of an English generation should be killed in this way.

The living and the dead: they were about the best crowd of people I ever knew, and I felt very sad at having to part from them.

I flew north in very bad weather and landed near Oxford in order to refuel. After taking off again, I flew towards the east, as the clouds were a little higher there, and I hit the L.N.E.R. line at Peterborough and came up the railway via Grantham, Doncaster, and Wakefield.

I circled over Glenwood and did one or two rolls till I saw somebody waving from the lawn, and then I flew off to Yeadon, where Father met me shortly afterwards. We drove over to Huddersfield and went straight to the nursing home.

I walked into the room and there were Dorothy and Nicholas waiting for me.

Also available in ISIS Large Print:

Sippers & Gulpers

Gordon Turner

"We all slept like logs until about 6 o'clock, when we were fully awakened by a small-size brass band, including drums and trumpets, playing America the Brave, which marched straight through the bedroom just to impress us 'limeys'!"

Having grown up in sleepy Swindon, Gordon Turner finds his eyes boggling as he enters New York Harbour on his way to pick up LST 406, the vessel that will be his home for the final four years of the Second World War. Follow Gordon's wonder of seeing North America before playing his part in the great landings of Sicily, Salerno, Anzio and Normandy. He relates his trials and tribulations of keeping body and soul together in the belly of this vast ship, including how he dealt with a complete dinner service of Naval china, having smuggled it off the LST.

ISBN 978-0-7531-9526-0 (hb)
ISBN 978-0-7531-9527-7 (pb)

RAF Liberator Over the Eastern Front

Jim Auton

"At our age, nobody would have allowed us to drive a car, borrow a motorbike or vote, but the Royal Air Force offered us the chance to leave home and fly an aeroplane. So we were hooked."

In 1941, Jim Auton enlisted in the wartime RAF as a pupil pilot. On learning that Air Bombers, a new category of aircrew, were serving as bomb aimers and co-pilots he opted for that role instead. Eventually he arrived in the south Italian war zone, flying B24 Liberators over dangerous targets such as Munich. Jim was severely wounded, and his flying career ended when he was only 20.

After the war, Jim set up a number of successful businesses with contacts in Communist controlled countries. This brought him to the attention of the Secret Services. He was ordered to become a spy but refused, with dire consequences. In his memoirs, Jim shares some of his most exciting ventures.

ISBN 978-0-7531-9520-8 (hb)
ISBN 978-0-7531-9521-5 (pb)

Mosquito Victory

Jack Currie

I levelled the Mosquito out at twenty-thousand feet, and gently tipped the right wing down. The lumps and hollows of the Cotswolds swung slowly round the long, smooth cowling of the starboard Merlin.

Jack Currie graphically describes the life of a wartime RAF bomber pilot on "rest", first instructing trainees on the four-engined Halifax bomber then later training as a glider pilot. He returned to operations with the Pathfinder force flying Mosquitoes of the 1409 Weather Flight. He was awarded the DFC in 1944, and was flying Mosquitoes when the war in Europe ended.

ISBN 978-0-7531-9516-1 (hb)
ISBN 978-0-7531-9517-8 (pb)

On and Off the Flight Deck

Henry "Hank" Adlam

"We had seen enough now to know that we would be lucky, either one of us, to see the end of the war and the future was always a taboo subject with any of us."

Hank Adlam began his naval flying career in January 1941 when he entered the flying course at Gosport naval barracks. Subsequently, on completion of flying training at Netheravon, he was selected as a fighter pilot and moved to the fighter school at Yeovilton. He took part in operations against the enemy from two Escort Carriers and one Fleet Carrier in the Atlantic, Arctic, Mediterranean and Far Eastern theatres of war. He went on to fly in operations against the Japanese in 1945, helping with the American battle for Okinawa.

His book is not about heroes and leaders of naval air warfare, although he points out that there were many of them, but a portrayal of an average young man, anxious to fight for his country, but having to cope with the tension of warfare.

ISBN 978-0-7531-9494-2 (hb)
ISBN 978-0-7531-9495-9 (pb)

The Tartan Pimpernel

Donald Caskie

"I had caught up with a struggling mass of people when German and Italian aircraft streaked down from the sky. Machine guns spat indiscriminate death. Bombs thudded and exploded all along the road."

This is the remarkable story of Donald Caskie, minister of the Scots Kirk in Paris at the time of the German invasion of France in 1940. Although he had several opportunities to flee, Caskie stayed behind to help establish a network of safe houses and escape routes for Allied soldiers and airmen trapped in occupied territory. This was dangerous work, and despite the constant threat of capture and execution, Caskie showed enormous resourcefulness and courage as he aided thousands of servicemen to freedom.

Finally arrested and interrogated, he was sentenced to death at a Nazi show trial, and it was only through the intervention of a German pastor that his life was saved.

ISBN 978-0-7531-9496-6 (hb)
ISBN 978-0-7531-9497-3 (pb)

ISIS publish a wide range of books in large print, from fiction to biography. Any suggestions for books you would like to see in large print or audio are always welcome. Please send to the Editorial Department at:

ISIS Publishing Limited
7 Centremead
Osney Mead
Oxford OX2 0ES

A full list of titles is available free of charge from:

Ulverscroft Large Print Books Limited

(UK)
The Green
Bradgate Road, Anstey
Leicester LE7 7FU
Tel: (0116) 236 4325

(Australia)
P.O. Box 314
St Leonards
NSW 1590
Tel: (02) 9436 2622

(USA)
P.O. Box 1230
West Seneca
N.Y. 14224-1230
Tel: (716) 674 4270

(Canada)
P.O. Box 80038
Burlington
Ontario L7L 6B1
Tel: (905) 637 8734

(New Zealand)
P.O. Box 456
Feilding
Tel: (06) 323 6828

Details of **ISIS** complete and unabridged audio books are also available from these offices. Alternatively, contact your local library for details of their collection of **ISIS** large print and unabridged audio books.